Praise Now!

Ready-to-Use Services for Contemporary Worship

Lynn Hurst
Sherrell Boles

Abingdon Press
Nashville

PRAISE NOW! READY TO USE SERVICES FOR CONTEMPORARY WORSHIP

Copyright © 2000 by Abingdon Press

This book is printed on acid-free, recycled paper.

ISBN 0-687-09080-6

A very special thank you
to Susan Fortune for the design and creation of the altars.
She graciously gives numerous hours to the task
of visually depicting the Word.
Each altar is a beautiful gift to God and our congregation.

---

04 05 06 07 08 09 — 10 9 8 7 6 5 4 3

MANUFACTURED IN THE UNITED STATES OF AMERICA

Contents

How to Use This Book

Overview

There are twenty thematic services included in this book. Each service is listed in the contents by its theme and title, with the scripture reference. The format for each service is as follows:

1. Theme, scripture, title, and specific time of the church year
2. A script with the order and approximate times for each component of worship
3. A list of the music resources used in the service
4. Skits and liturgies written for each specific service
5. A description and picture of the altar (picture printed elsewhere by the title)
6. Suggested resources for music, recordings, dramas, and movies
7. A sermon guide

Explanation

In planning this contemporary worship experience, a thematic (sometimes following the lectionary) approach is used. It is very important to the visionaries of this service that while the design should be innovative and experiential, it also should be distinctly United Methodist. We do not want to forget our heritage and therefore need to incorporate a strong sense of who we are as United Methodists in this contemporary setting. Additionally, there are many worship resources published that you may want to consider when reviewing these services for use in your ministry setting.

We believe that the style of these services goes beyond the praise and worship style found in most contemporary settings. A praise and worship style uses a large portion of the time to sing choruses that are not necessarily chosen for their thematic content, and there is usually little or no liturgy.

Each of these services has been designed so that the worshiper will experience God's Word, which addresses the chosen theme, from the beginning to the end of the service. The theme is chosen for its relevance to our current world. The worshiper should experience the Word in as many ways as possible (i.e., using all the five senses). It is our desire that as the worshiper enters the worship space and sees the altar, he or she will begin to sense what the theme of the service might be. This style of service is appealing to the well-seasoned worshiper as well as to the nonbeliever.

The times listed are approximate but will aid you in making any necessary adjustments to your service. The abbreviation **WL** stands for Worship Leader (the person or persons designated to lead the congregation through the service). The abbreviation **PT** stands for Praise Team (the singers and instrumentalists leading in worship).

Who will be leading your worship? There are many possible combinations that you might use. One option is to use a man and woman team as the worship leaders along with two to four back-up singers. The band could include a drummer, a bass guitarist, additional guitarists, saxophones or other instruments, and a keyboardist. All these people make up the praise team, but the **PT** abbreviations found in these scripts usually apply only to the praise team singers. You might choose to use only one worship leader (man or woman) with a larger backup group. Also, you might have a contemporary choir as backup and for special music. Your praise band can consist of any combination of instruments with which you have to work. Most contemporary music resources now have instrumental books written to supplement the songbook.

There are a few components of worship that have not been addressed in these scripts. You will need to consider the following:

1. Will you have prelude music, and if so, what type? Whether live or recorded music is used, try to choose music that reflects the theme of the service. If the praise band plays, plan to use a combination of songs that are in the script.
2. Do you need to have a time for church announcements? Often it is best to make any

necessary announcements before the service begins. Also, creative announcement slides can be run prior to the service. If you need to make announcements later in the service, be sensitive to the flow of the service.

3. How will you receive the offering? Be sensitive to the flow of the service. Try to avoid sticking it in just to take the offering. Use it as a part of the service to depict the theme, to teach the congregation about the purpose of the offering, to respond to the sermon, and so forth. Make it a meaningful time of the service. When communion is served, people can bring their offering forward as they come to take communion.

4. Use several different methods of serving communion if it is possible to do so in your setting. When communion is not the same old routine, it takes on new meaning. The amount of creativity you can use for serving communion will be dependent upon the size of your congregation. Consider serving twelve people at a time while they are seated at a table in the center of the room. On another occasion, the communion liturgy may be performed in mime, and then the mimes can serve communion to the congregation.

You may want to use these services in their entirety, or you may simply take bits and pieces from them to design your own service. In either case, we hope the uniqueness of each service will spark your creativity.

Music Resources ♫

All music resources are noted by an icon. See page 85 for a complete list.

Licenses Needed

The largest licensing agency is Christian Copyright Licensing, Inc. The license covers more than 100,000 songs from more than 2,000 publishers and songwriters. After paying an annual fee, your church will receive a license with your "SongSelect Activation Code" printed on it. This is the number that you must display on all copies you make. You will also receive a current License Manual that will be your resource for all the songs that can be used. The cost to your church is based on your church's average weekly worship attendance for all services.

Your active license grants you permission to:
• Print song and hymn **texts** in bulletins, programs, liturgies, and song sheets.
• Create overhead transparencies, slides, or use any other format whereby song **texts** are visually projected, such as computer graphics and projection.
• Arrange, print, and copy your own vocal or instrumental arrangements of songs, where no published version is available.
• Record your worship services by audio or video means, provided you only record "live" music (instrumental and vocal). Accompaniment tracks cannot be reproduced. Information concerning fees you may charge and other information is available from the company.

Your active license does *not* grant you permission to:
• Photocopy or duplicate octavos, cantatas, musicals, handbell music, keyboard arrangements, vocal scores, orchestrations, or other instrumental works.
• Translate songs from English into another language. This can only be done with the approval of the respective copyright administrator.
• Rent, sell, lend, or distribute copies made under the Church Copyright License to individuals or groups outside the church, or to other churches.
• Assign or transfer the Church Copyright License to any other church or group without CCLI's approval.

Christian Copyright Licensing, Inc. (CCLI)
17201 N.E. Sacramento
Portland, OR 97230
Call: 1-800-234-2446
E-mail: support@ccli.com
Internet: www.ccli.com

The U.S. Copyright Act also states that all home videocassettes shown outside one's personal residence are "public performances," and mandates that they be licensed. Noncompliance with the law is subject to statutory damages starting at $500 per exhibition. This legal requirement applies equally to profit and non-profit facilities, whether or not an admission is charged. The Motion Picture Licensing Corporation (MPLC), the authorized licensing agent for Hollywood studios and producers ranging from Disney to Warner Brothers, provides the necessary public performance license so you can comply with the Federal Copyright Law. The MPLC offers a renewable, annual license for $95 per congregation. Public performances may take place only at the location you specify on your license. The license doesn't cover advertising specific titles to the general public or charging a fee to view them.

The Motion Picture Licensing Corporation
5455 Centinela Ave.
P.O. Box 66970
Los Angeles, CA 90066-6970
Call: 1-800-462-8855
Fax: 1-310-822-4440

Looking for movie clips for your service?

The Internet Movie Database
Internet: http://us.imdb.com
    This free database aims to capture any and all information associated with movies from across the world, from the earliest cinema to the very latest releases. Thousands of films are catalogued here, making it an amazingly comprehensive reference. It has a powerful search tool that allows you to key in plot summaries, character names, movie ratings, titles, key words or quotes, and much more. It is the closest thing to a "motion picture concordance" available.

Altar Supplies
    The following are suggested items to have in your basic altar "pantry":
1. Six to ten yards of fabrics in liturgical colors (white, purple, green, and red). Use quality polyester that will not wrinkle and will drape well. Consider adding aqua-colored fabric to use as the symbol of water, and black fabric for Good Friday or the beginning of your Easter service. These fabrics can be used as filler around objects on the altar, as a part of the design, or as flowing connectors from the altar to the congregation.
2. Tulle (extra fine net). Tulle is wonderful to work with in designing an altar. You will not want to use it every week, but it will add a beautiful dimension to your design on occasion. I recommend purchasing ten yards of white, red, and aqua. Do **not** place tulle too close to lighted candles since it ignites easily.
3. Candles in different sizes, shapes, and colors. It is also helpful to have candleholders of various styles: gold finish, black iron, and earthenware.
4. Wicker baskets in different sizes and shapes, and glass bowls.
5. Silk ivy, ferns, and filler. Artificial greenery can be rather expensive, but it adds so much to the creation of a complete design. Plants will be used quite often and are, therefore, well worth the expense.
6. Other unusual items. Collect sticks from yards, rocks from a river bottom, seashells, and any other items you think might be used. You never know what will spark your creativity!

A lot of these items are used numerous times throughout the year. A few other items that will not be used as often are:
1. A running water fountain
2. Hurricane lamps
3. Artificial white doves
4. Floating candles
5. Mexican-style blankets
6. A gold triangle
7. Advent wreath

Interpretive Dance
    You can begin with one dancer or a group of dancers but in either case, good leadership should be developed. High school girls/boys in classical ballet could be beginning leaders as well as an adult or group of adults who studied dance throughout high school. The dancers should have a concept of stage presence and how to interpret with fluid body movements. Dancers that have been classically trained should be able to develop liturgical dance with confidence. If you are unable to recruit trained dancers with which to begin, take a group of people to several workshops where they can observe different styles of interpretive dance for

worship. Most worship/music events incorporate interpretive dance in their training events. Consider the following when including interpretive dance in your worship service:

- What is to be interpreted? Music? Scripture? Liturgy? Sermon? Communion?
- How many people will be used? A solo can be just as effective as a large group of people. If a larger group is needed, should both male and female and different age people used?
- Will props be needed? Items are quite often used in the interpretation and placed on the altar. Some possibilities are candles, scarves, banners, and communion elements.
- What will be the appropriate attire? Ask dance teachers to make recommendations and to share their dance catalogs with you. Make sure that what you choose is church appropriate for your congregation.
- How much rehearsal will be required? With experienced dancers, two rehearsals will be needed—one for choreography and one for run through. You will need to allow for more rehearsals for the inexperienced.

If simply choreographed and well rehearsed, interpretive dance will become a very powerful and meaningful part of your service.

Drama Resources

As in dance, leadership will need to be developed for a drama team. Look for a person who is a drama major or a leader in Community Theater. These persons almost always want another venue in which to use their skills. There are numerous resources to help the amateur develop a drama team with professional results. The following are a few good examples:

Drama Ministry (How to Produce and Direct Effective Drama in Your Worship Services) This is a very good resource published eight times a year. Contact: Communication Resources, Inc.
4150 Belden Village St., 4th floor
Canton, OH 44718
1-800-98-DRAMA
Fax: 1-330-493-3158
E-Mail: Drama@ComResources.com
www.DramaMinistry.com

Drama for Worship Volumes 1-8
Distributed by Word, Inc.
Call: 1-800-251-4000

The Worship Drama Library
Lillenas Publishing Co.
Kansas City, MO 64101
Nine volumes with twelve dramas each; listed by topic. Permission to copy for local use.

Cross Point Scripts
Communication Resources
(see above)
Fifty scripts, including sketches, readers theater and mime; indexed by scripture text and related topics/themes

Sunday Morning Live from Willow Creek Community Church
Willow Creek Resources/Zondervan
Call: 1-800-876-7335
Fax: 1-610-532-9001
www.zondervan.com
Each volume includes six reproducible sketches. A video of each is available.

Consider the following when using drama in the worship service:

- A short sketch can be used almost every week in one of the following ways: to set up the theme for the service; as a Call to Worship; to set up the sermon; as a time of reflection at the end of the service.
- A longer drama can be used as the body of the service.
- Mime can be used to illustrate the sermon or to set up communion.
- How much rehearsal will be needed? One time will probably suffice for a short sketch but more time will be needed depending on the complexity and length of the drama.
- Quite often it is much more effective to write your own dramatic sketch based upon the theme of the service and the development of the sermon.

Preaching Helps

Contemporary worship is more than just upbeat music and the preacher preaching without notes. In developing these contemporary worship services, the theme of the service directs everything into a balanced whole. The service becomes the proclamation of the Word with the sermon being only one piece of the whole. The preacher should not formulate the sermon in isolation and then hope that the sermon and music fit. It is helpful for the preacher and other worship leaders to work together to develop a theme so that the Word is proclaimed at every point in the service. The synergy that comes from this team effort will become essential in sermon development.

The preaching notes in this book are by no means the sermon in its entirety. The notes give the reader a general synopsis of the sermon based on the theme of the service.

The sermon section begins with the Idea Generator to help stimulate the preacher to focus spiritually on the theme of the week as well as offer suggestions on how to apply the theme in the context of one's own ministry. It is hoped that this section will offer an opportunity for the preacher to develop additional illustrations with the Idea Generator as a type of conversation partner. Because we believe that our worship should be meaningful in addressing the life situations of the people in our congregations, the Idea Generator combines the heart of pastoral care with meditative exercises.

You will notice that the sermons are not designed in one format. The challenge is to allow one to experiment with different formats and styles. Surprisingly, we have found that for the people who are drawn to this experiential type of service, a teaching style of sermon is very appealing. Many times we have used an outline that was incorporated into the Power Point (visual) presentation. We also gave out copies of the outline to each one present allowing room between major points for notations to be made. The congregational response to this type of format has been very positive.

Also, we have experimented with first-person sermons, sermons drawn from the responses of the congregation, and sermons developed through video presentations. We have included some of these in the book and made notes as needed in how the Word was proclaimed through these various techniques.

There is no exegetical material included in the sermon section. However, the sermons are developed through strong exegetical methods. There are many good resources for exegesis that the preacher probably has in his or her own library. The Internet is an excellent resource for exegetical research as well as for the development of many of the illustrations that you will find in these sermons. (See page 85 for a list of Internet Resources.)

Conclusion

Worship is more than one hour of singing, preaching, scripture, and an offering. We believe that worship is experiencing and praising God every day of our lives. These services can be a catalyst to live a worship-filled life. "I appeal to you therefore, brothers and sisters, by the mercies of God, to present your bodies as a living sacrifice, holy and acceptable to God, which is your spiritual worship" (Rom. 12:1). Our prayer is that your community of faith will be blessed and will grow in faith as you worship together.

Living Water

Communion

(10 min.) **Pastor:** Welcome/Announcements/**Skit #1:** *I'm Thirsty*

WL: Lead Call to Worship.
1. "Sing Unto the Lord" (unknown) SFPW, 23
2. "The Joy of the Lord" (Vale) SFPW, 229
3. "Jesus Is My Lord" (unknown) SFPW, 54

PT: The first scripture reading—John 4:5-15

(All three scripture readings in this service are presented by three readers: Jesus, woman, and narrator.)

(10 min.) **Pastor:** Sermon Segment #1 ("We Need Water!")

PT: The second scripture reading—John 4:16-27

Skit #2: *Take a Drink*

(10 min.) **Pastor:** Sermon Segment #2 ("We Get Water From Unexpected Places.")

PT: The third scripture reading—John 4:28-30, 39-42

Skit #3: *Overflowing Water*

(5 min.) **Pastor:** Sermon segment #3 ("Water Demands to Be Given!")

(10 min.) **Communion**
4. "You Who Are Thirsty" (Ross) SFPW, 219
5. "I Love You, Lord" (Klein) SFPW, 72
6. "Sanctuary" (Thompson/Scruggs) CCB, 87
7. "Fill My Cup, Lord" (Blanchard) UMH, 641

(10 min.) **Pastor:** Lead congregational prayer time.

WL: Lead closing song. *(During the song, ushers hand each person a small empty cup to take home.)*
8. "Come Just As You Are" (Sabolick) PHC, 179

Pastor: Benediction

Music Sources: *Songs for Praise and Worship* (Word); *Cokesbury Chorus Book* (Abingdon Press); *Praise Hymns & Choruses* (Maranatha); *The United Methodist Hymnal* (UMPH).

SKIT #1: *I'm Thirsty*

At the conclusion of the announcements, the pastor asks someone in the congregation to bring him or her a drink of water. *(This should be prearranged.)* While waiting on the clear glass of water, the pastor simply hums "Fill My Cup, Lord." Upon receiving the water, the pastor raises the glass for all to see, takes a drink and says, "Yes, that was just what I needed."

CALL TO WORSHIP

L: Sometimes our souls are like dry desert places.

P: Give us water to drink.

L: Sometimes our spirits are withering on the vine.

P: Give us water to drink.

L: Sometimes our bodies need restoration and refreshment.

P: Give us water to drink.

L: Jesus said, "I am the living water. Whoever drinks of my water will never be thirsty again."

P: Jesus, give us this water so that we will never be thirsty.

SKIT #2: *Take a Drink*
(A man and a woman)

(The man enters first, with a cup of water in hand, and is seated on a park bench. He is Mr. Cheerful about everything and is humming "Fill My Cup, Lord." The woman enters as Mrs. Grump, with book in hand, and is seated next to the man. After a few seconds of looking at the book, she throws it on the ground.)

Man: *(Reaches down to pick up the book.)* "The Miraculous Cure for All Your Problems" . . . interesting title . . . did it work?

Woman: Not really. I still feel like my prayers are hitting the ceiling. I have no real direction in my life . . . I feel drained, dried up . . . I feel thirsty.

Man: *(Continues humming and offers the woman his cup of water.)*

Woman: No, no . . . you misunderstood. I didn't mean that I am literally thirsty.

Man: *(With a smile)* I know. *(Hands her the cup of water again.)*

(They both freeze in position for a few seconds, then move back to their places.)

SKIT #3: *Overflowing Water*
(This skit requires four people: A leader to pour water and the other three to receive it.)

(The leader picks up the pitcher of water and motions to the first person as if he or she wants to give that person some water. Person #1 picks up a cup and holds it out for the leader to pour into the cup. The leader begins humming "Fill My Cup, Lord." The water gets close to the top.)

Person #1: Wait, wait . . . it's going to overflow!

Leader: I know. It's living water.

(As the water is overflowing, Person #1 motions for Person #2 to help. Person #2 picks up a cup and holds it under #1's cup to catch the overflow. Person #1 moves to the side and begins humming "Fill My Cup, Lord" with the leader. When #2's cup is full, he or she motions for #3 to come catch the overflow. Person #3 puts a cup under #2's cup and #2 moves to the side and begins humming with the others. When #3's cup is full and everyone is humming, all four should lift cups high and begin singing the words to "Fill My Cup, Lord.")

COMMUNION LITURGY

Living God, you meet us at the point of our need—when we are thirsty, when our souls feel like a dry parched land. You quench us with the water that leaves us satisfied. Even on the most difficult night with your disciples, you reminded them that you are the substance of life. You took bread and broke it, gave it to your disciples and said, "This is my body." Then you took the cup and blessed it and gave it to your disciples and said, "This is my blood—do this in remembrance of me." Just as the disciples experienced grace unexpectedly, we too, receive grace unexpectedly. Through your sacrifice of body and blood, we are assured of life eternal. Pour out your Holy Spirit on this bread and wine. May it be for us the body and blood of Christ, that we may be the body of Christ in the world.

Empower us to be a witness of the living water. Amen.

BENEDICTION

Pastor: *(Holds up empty cup.)* You are going to meet someone this week who is empty. Let this empty cup be a reminder that you have received living water. Thank you, Lord, for your living water that demands to be given. Hallelujah, Amen

ALTAR

A white cloth covers the altar. Ten yards of silklike aqua fabric is draped from the center music stand, under the running water fountain on top of the altar, and over a small table in front of the altar. The fabric should continue to flow into the center aisle as far as possible. This should give the effect of a waterfall. A blue bowl is placed on the small table for people to place their offerings or prayer cards in when they come forward for communion. Three small blue votive candles are in front of the water fountain. The communion bread is on the left side of the water fountain with grapes around the base of the bread. The communion cups are on the right side with grapes at the base. Silk ferns are used as the backdrop.

OPTIONS

Music ♫
"All You Who Are Thirsty" (Connolly) *Come Celebrate!* (Abingdon Press)
"Come to the Table" (Cloninger/Nystrom) *Praise Worship Songbook #6* (Integrity)
"One Bread, One Body" (Foley) *The United Methodist Hymnal* (UMPH)
"Water of Life" (Townley) *Come Celebrate!* (Abingdon Press)

Recordings 📼
Living Water, Bread of Life as performed by 4 Him, from *4 Him* (Benson Records)

SERMON 📖

Idea Generator
Americans and people in other developed countries often take fresh water for granted. But when a disaster occurs in which the fresh water supply is affected, we suddenly realize the necessity of fresh water. Our spiritual lives are also subject to dry periods, and often in times of spiritual disasters we suddenly experience the desolation of our own dry souls. We have taken for granted the life-giving water.

The spiritual exercise for this service might be an opportunity for the pastor and worship leaders to survey how the living water of Jesus is shared with the congregation. One of the key factors is an examination by the worship leaders of their own individual lives. It is very easy for those leading worship to be so busy trying to share the living water that in the process they forget to return to the source of living water to be replenished.

How do the worship leaders prepare both individually and corporately for worship? Where do they have the space and opportunity to worship and share with others? These are important questions we must ask to ensure that our water supply is fresh and life-giving. Wouldn't it be tragic if we died of thirst because of neglect of our own need for nourishment? Wouldn't it be even more tragic if those who depend on us died with us because we neglected our own spirituality? We cannot give that which we do not possess. We have a wonderful opportunity to lead worship, but with opportunity comes responsibility. Let us be faithful in this responsibility.

(This sermon has been divided into three segments. See script.)

Segment #1: "We Need Water"
Imagine a hot day. The sun is beating down on you. Your mouth is dry and your tongue feels thick. Wouldn't a cool glass of water be just perfect right now? But wait, you realize that you are on a raft drifting on an ocean. All around you is water. But, there is a problem. The ocean water is undrinkable because it is salt water. You need fresh water.

In the summer of 1999, a news article reported that seawater, which contains salt, was threatening municipal water supplies in some eastern communities where there had been substantial drought. The Hudson and Delaware Rivers were being monitored for saltwater encroachment. The threat of salt water contamination to the fresh water supply brings a host of problems; the most serious concern is that our bodies cannot absorb salt water properly.

We need fresh water. Water is the most important molecule on the earth. We can live without food for several weeks, but we can live only a few days without water. Nearly 60 percent of our body weight is water. The human body needs approximately eight glasses of water daily.

Jesus meets a woman who is not aware of her need for the living water. Like a person drifting in the ocean, she has surrounded herself with what appears to be the life-giving water only to find out through her conversation with Jesus that it is salt water. And just like the water from the ocean, this salt water is potentially dangerous. Jesus helps her to recognize her need for fresh water. But where can she get this water?

Segment #2: "We Get Water From Unexpected Places"

If this woman had been asked before she met Jesus if she would find fulfillment for her thirsty soul through an encounter with a traveling Jewish rabbi, she would probably have been incredulous. Jews and Samaritans did not associate with each other and had some significant theological differences. It would require her moving out of her comfort zone to be in conversation with someone like Jesus. And yet, water is found in unexpected places.

When I was a child, my family used to stop at a roadside diner as we traveled to visit my grandparents. Outside the diner was a fountain that was built into boulders along the road. It looked as if water were actually coming out of the rock. No matter how many times we stopped I never tired of this amazing sight. This is water from an unexpected source.

Many times we have built up our defenses and the usual avenues of water are closed to us because the pipes are rusty. Jesus surprises us by building new waterways.

Segment #3: "Water Demands to Be Given"

We miss an essential component if we don't listen to the story in its entirety. Jesus offered this woman an opportunity to partake of the living water, but it didn't stop there. This kind of water has to be shared. It cannot be hoarded or stored for rainy days because it will become stagnant.

Have you ever seen water that has no place to run off? It becomes stagnant—a breeding ground for disease. Have you ever turned on a faucet connected to a well? If the water has been shut off for any period of time, it becomes stale and can even have an unpleasant odor until it is allowed to run freely for awhile.

The Samaritan woman shared with the community the water she had been given and in turn *her* water became *their* water. As a community of faith, we meet people every day who need this living water. I once heard the community of faith described as beggars who are showing other beggars where to find bread. Perhaps we could also describe the community of faith as thirsty people who have discovered a fresh water supply after drifting on the salty ocean. In giving the water away, we discover our own supply is never-ending.

NOTES_____

_____

_____

_____

_____

_____

_____

_____

_____

_____

_____

Alternative Lifestyle

Ordinary Time

(10 min.)   **Pastor:** Read John 10:1-10 from *THE MESSAGE* (Eugene Peterson)

Call to Worship Skit: *The Sheep Rustler*

(10 min.)   **PT:** Lead the opening songs.

> 1. "Like a Shepherd" (Moen/Simpson) C&W, 112

WL or Pastor: Lead Call to Worship.

> 2. "I Will Celebrate" (Duvall) SFPW, 147

> 3. "Jehovah-Jireh" (Watson) SFPW, 228

WL: Lead unison Invocation.

> 4. "Antiphonal Praise" (Green) SFPW, 25

> 5. "In His Presence" (Tunney) SFPW, 46

Pastor: Lead congregational prayer time.

(20 min.)   **Pastor:** Sermon

(15 min.)   Special music while the offering is being received.

Solo: "The Lord Is My Shepherd" (Townley) CC, 15

Response to the Word: Ask for brief witnesses from the congregation about what has spoken to them this week or today as they heard the Word. *(Allow ten minutes for these personal responses.)*

PT: Lead the closing song.
> 6. "Jehovah-Jireh" (Watson) SFPW, 228

Pastor: Benediction

Music Sources: *Come & Worship* (Integrity); *Songs for Praise & Worship* (Word); *Come Celebrate!* (Abingdon Press)

CALL TO WORSHIP SKIT: *The Sheep Rustler*

(Six people from the congregation should be chosen ahead of time to participate in this skit. The first three will simply remain in their seats while the next three will get up from their seats and follow Jesus. Only Jesus and the sheep rustler have spoken lines.)

(The sheep rustler can be dressed in appropriate attire with a lasso, if possible. Jesus should wear a biblical costume and carry a shepherd's crook. As the sheep rustler enters, have the PT Band play background music. The rustler is trying to lure each person from their seat to follow him or her.)

Rustler: *(To Person #1)* I know you would like to sleep late. God wants you to rest on the Sabbath. Trust me—nobody will miss you if you are not here.

(To Person #2) I know you would like to be out on the golf course. Isn't there something in the Bible about the green pastures?

(To Person #3) I bet you would like a sports utility vehicle. Well, go right ahead and get it. God owns everything. Do you think he needs your money?

Jesus: *(Moves to each person and touches him or her on the shoulder.)*
(To Person #1) [Name], I need you to follow me.
(To Person #2) [Name], I can give you everything you need.
(To Person #3) [Name], come, follow me.

(Each person gets up and follows Jesus down the aisle.)

CALL TO WORSHIP
L: We all want the abundant life.
P: But what is the abundant life?
L: Some say that the abundant life is health, wealth, and happiness.
P: Is that really the abundant life?
L: Jesus said that the abundant life is life with him forever.

INVOCATION
Holy God, we confess that it is hard for us to be still and rest in your holy presence. We long to clear our minds of our hectic lifestyles and the temptations of the world around us. We desire the abundant life you offer and not the abundant life the world is selling.

Loving God, teach us how to come into your presence and how to remain in your presence all the days of our lives. Amen.

BENEDICTION
Jesus said, "My sheep know my voice." Do you know his voice? Is your lifestyle a reflection of one who knows Jesus' voice? Are you living the abundant life? He has come that we might have the abundant life with him forever. Hallelujah, Amen.

ALTAR
Silk ferns and ivy cover the top of the altar to give a plush, green pasture effect. A single white candle inside a hurricane lamp is placed in the center to represent Christ. Pink geraniums are interspersed in the green pasture for color.

OPTIONS

Music
"Hallowed Be Thy Name" (Mason/Lawson) *Songs for Praise & Worship* (Word)
"Oh, How He Loves You and Me" (Kaiser) *Songs for Praise & Worship* (Word)
"Shepherd of My Soul" (Nystrom) *Praise Hymns & Choruses (4th ed)* (Maranatha)
"The Lord Is Near" (Balhoff/Ducote/Daigle) *Come Celebrate!* (Abingdon Press)
"The Steadfast Love of the Lord" (McNeill) *Songs for Praise & Worship* (Word)
"Think About His Love" (Harrah) *Come & Worship* (Integrity)
"You Have Been Good" (Paris) *Songs for Praise & Worship* (Word)
"Your Mercy Flows" (Sutton) *Songs for Praise & Worship* (Word)

Recordings
"Find Me" as performed by Margaret Becker, from *The Reckoning* and *Steps of Faith* (Sparrow Records)
"Living Water, Bread of Life" as performed by 4 Him, from *4 Him* (Benson Records)

"More to This Life" as performed by Steven
  Curtis Chapman, from *More to This Life*
  (Sparrow Records)
"Who Makes the Rules" as performed by Steven
  Curtis Chapman, from *More to This Life*
  (Sparrow Records)

SERMON

Idea Generator

What images does the phrase "abundant
life" provoke in your congregation? In a society
driven by Madison Avenue hype, it might seem
that abundant life is found in the abundance of
one's lifestyle. You will probably have a variety
of income levels in your congregation. When
you think about the lifestyles of the members of
your congregation, do they reflect abundance as
defined by the culture? This is not an exercise
in judgment because we as pastors can easily
find ourselves in the same cultural abundance
mind-set. (Isn't it wonderful to pastor a large-
steeple church with influential people in the
community? It is a good professional move to
accept significant leadership positions in most
denominations.)

We can have everything and still live an
impoverished, sad spiritual life. How can we
address this in our message? Perhaps one place
to start is by looking at Jesus' words and making
a list of how Jesus defines the abundant life.
What is Jesus' value system and how does ours
compare?

Introduction

Once, when I was coming back from a business trip, I got bumped up from economy to
first class for my flight home. I really enjoyed
the experience. This was the abundant life.
Being served food on real china, sitting in a
roomy seat, and getting special attention by the
flight attendants was very delightful. I wanted to
be able to fly first class all the time. I didn't
want to go back to economy. I liked living this
abundant life.

Body

In the world, there is a growing distance
between the two spectrums of the economic
scale. People are driven to be successful so that
they may be on the upper end of that scale. Our
eyes and ears are assaulted every day through
television and media with what is needed to
have the abundant life. We are told that everything from the car we drive to the toothpaste we
use is essential for having an abundant life.

But, like the sheep rustler in Jesus' story,
this surface-glitzy lifestyle is really a bandit or
thief. This lifestyle suggests to us that our wealth
and fame will satisfy us, but then we find ourselves in a death trap. The thief comes to steal,
kill, and destroy. This pseudo-abundant life
seems to be fulfilling until a crisis occurs. Then
we find the fake abundant life doesn't have any
substance. It sparkles and glitters like fool's gold
but when it is needed to back up our life, it falls
apart.

Jesus offers us a promise of abundant life,
which means a life beyond measure. There are
two images of Jesus that are at the heart of
understanding abundant life. The most obvious
is the shepherd, but Jesus also describes himself
as the gate. Why this image? Perhaps the image
helps us to understand that abundant life is
found in who Jesus is and our relationship with
him.

Conclusion

I confessed how comfortable it was to fly
first-class, but it is important to know the flight
home eventually ended. My abundant life was
only temporary, but the abundant life offered
by Jesus is permanent. He has come that we
might have life and have it abundantly in our
relationship with him.

NOTES_____

_____

_____

_____

_____

_____

_____

_____

Got Peace?

Communion

(10 min.) **Pastor:** Welcome/announcements/end announcement time by saying,
"We'll be right back after this commercial message."

Call to Worship Skit: *Got Peace?*

(5 min.)   **WL:** Lead Call to Worship.
1. "I Will Enter His Gates" (Brethorst) SFPW, 168
2. "We Bring the Sacrifice of Praise" (Dearman) SFPW, 1
3. "Ah, Lord God" (Chance) SFPW, 2

(10 min.) **WL or Soloist:** Words of preparation for prayer followed by first
verse of "Near to the Heart of God" (McAfee) UMH, 472

Pastor: Lead prayer time followed by congregational response.
4. "Near to the Heart of God" (vs. 3) UMH, 472

WL: Lead responsive scripture reading (Phil. 4:4-7).
5. "He Is Our Peace" (Groves) PHC, 32
6. "My Peace" (Routledge) PHC, 53

(20 min.) **Band:** Continue to play as **PT** is seated. Fade music out as movie clip
begins (*Twister*, Warner Brothers Films).
Description: Bill and Jo are chasing a tornado.
Start Time: 31:34
Start Cue: Bill: "This was a great idea!"
End Time: 33:17
End Cue: Tornado passes over bridge and Jo looks out at the destruction.

Pastor: Sermon
I. We need a foundation.
II. We need to be prepared.
III. We need to embrace life.
IV. Got Peace? Yeah!

(10 min.) *(Begin soft background music [recorded or live] while showing peaceful scenes on screen. Invite someone to light the candles on the altar. Lower volume of music as the pastor gives the words of consecra-
tion. Share communion in your faith tradition. Continue peaceful music during communion. Offerings
may be brought forward during communion.)*

(5 min.)   **PT:** Lead closing song.

WL or Pastor: Offer a time of commitment.
7. "Let the Peace of Christ Rule in Your Heart" (Cagle) SFPW, 251

WL or Pastor: Benediction

Music Sources: *Songs for Praise & Worship* (Word); *The United Methodist Hymnal* (UMPH); *Praise
Hymns & Choruses* (Maranatha)

CALL TO WORSHIP SKIT: *Got Peace?*

Characters:
  Salesperson: Man or woman with outgoing personality
  Man and **Woman:** Preferably married, with obvious differing opinions on the type of car needed
  Commercial Director: Man or woman

Band: Play upbeat background music similar to what is used in a car commercial as actors enter for the skit. A picture of a very expensive car should be displayed. At the end of the skit, the band should repeat the music that was played at the beginning as the PT moves into place.

(Man and Woman enter talking about finding the "perfect car" to buy.)

(Salesperson approaches and begins talking about selling them the car that will take them away to ultimate peace. It will be the answer to all their problems.)

Woman: You know, I have a deadline for a book I'm writing. I need to find a way to get peace and be undisturbed while I write.

Salesperson: I have just the car for you! You can find that peaceful place of quiet and no disruption because this car will take you anywhere!

Man: But I have back problems. It's hard for me to drive for any length of time. I can't get any peace with all the pain I have here. *(Points to his back.)*

Salesperson: Then this car is the one for you! It has a built-in massager that will do wonders for your back. It will relax you so much that you will feel total peace.

Woman: I certainly don't feel peaceful unless I can control my climate.

Salesperson: This car is perfect for you! It has automatic climate control. You can even set individual seat vents to your own preference. This will give peace to the traveling family.

Man: Speaking of traveling, there are so many new communities here in this area that I get lost when I am out visiting people. I'm late for appointments and sometimes can't even find the place I'm going. It sure would make my life more peaceful if I could find places easier.

Salesperson: That will never be a problem for you again in this car. It has a satellite tracking system for the whole country and even one for this city. Just type in the address and it will show you on the monitor the easiest route to your destination. It even gives alternate routes in case of road construction. The peace of mind you get will be worth the price.

Woman: You know, in this day and age, I don't feel safe. There is so much evil in the world: drive-by shootings, road rage, car theft, assaults, and who knows what else. Feeling peaceful when you're alone in a car is impossible.

Salesperson: This car can alleviate your worries. It has bulletproof glass, a super-sensitive alarm system and a one-button computer contact to emergency road service or 911.

Man: I just need a little peace and relaxation. My life is on such a fast pace that I feel like my head is going to explode.

Salesperson: We've got you covered there, too. This car is equipped with the latest sound system. Just pop in a relaxation tape and seal out all those outside disturbances. Guaranteed to make you sigh a peaceful sigh. And do you know what? All this can be yours for only $75,000!

Woman: This is the answer to all our problems and will give us the peace we are looking for. Where do we sign?

Commercial Director: Cut, cut! Thanks guys, this is really a great commercial. Just what we wanted!

Woman: *(To husband)* This is ridiculous! Would anyone really think that a car could solve all their problems and give them peace?

Man: I don't know, but we are paid to sell the car, not be spiritual guides.

Commercial Director: *(To congregation)* Got peace?

CALL TO WORSHIP
L: God, help us to have a foundation,
P: at all times!
L: Help us to be prepared,
P: at all times!
L: Help us to embrace life,
P: at all times!
L: Help us to be at peace,
P: at all times!

RESPONSIVE SCRIPTURE READING
L: Rejoice in the Lord always; and again I will say
P: Rejoice.
L: Let your gentleness be known to everyone.
P: The Lord is near.
L: Do not worry about anything, but in everything by prayer and supplication with thanksgiving let your requests be made known to God.
P: And the peace of God, which surpasses all understanding, will guard your hearts and your minds in Christ Jesus.

WORDS OF CONSECRATION
For the disciples, there was a storm coming. They didn't know it, but Christ knew it. So he offered them a foundation that would prepare them to face the storm with the assurance of life eternal. Christ has offered us that same foundation. Therefore, we can celebrate communion with that same assurance of life eternal. Jesus has prepared the way and embraces us with inner peace during our storms of life. *(Consecrate the communion elements in your tradition.)*

BENEDICTION
L: Do you have a firm foundation?
P: at all times!
L: Are you prepared for the storms of life?
P: at all times!
L: Do you embrace life?
P: at all times!
L: Got peace?
P: Yeah! Hallelujah, Amen!

ALTAR
A large, traditional gold cross with a white dove attached is in the center of the altar. In front of the cross is a white pillar candle. White fabric covers boxes of different heights on which grapes, ivy, and numerous candles are placed. The communion bread is on the right side of the altar and the juice is on the left side. White tulle is draped from the top of the cross, down the sides of the altar and to the floor.

OPTIONS

Music
"He Is Able" (Noland/Ferguson) *Praise Hymns & Choruses* (Maranatha)
"Hear My Prayer" (Owens) *Praise Hymns & Choruses* (Maranatha)
"It Is Well with My Soul" (Spafford/Bliss) *The United Methodist Hymnal* (UMPH)
"Rejoice, the Lord Is King" (Wesley/Handel) *The United Methodist Hymnal* (UMPH)
"Shepherd of My Soul" (Nystrom) *Praise Hymns & Choruses* (Maranatha)
"Still Waters" (Carroll) *Praise Hymns & Choruses* (Maranatha)

Recordings
"I Will Rest" as performed on *We Draw Near* with Marty Nystrom (Integrity)
"More to This Life" as performed by Steven Curtis Chapman from *More to This Life* (Sparrow Records)
"Rest" as performed by Denny Correll and the Maranatha! Singers, from *Praise 15, The Finale* (Maranatha! Records)

Movies
The tornado scene from *The Wizard of Oz*

SERMON

Idea Generator
A young mother is diagnosed with breast cancer; a teenager is arrested for DUI; a man loses his job of twenty years due to downsizing. Pastors encounter all these scenarios each week. Take a minute to jot down all the seemingly hopeless situations you have encountered over the last few weeks. How do we preach peace to our communities when so many will encounter a storm this year, this month, this day?

If you are not able to show the *Twister* segment as an introduction to your sermon, watch it at home in preparation for what is going on in people's lives. People need a word of hope on how to live in God's peace during the storm.

Introduction

Conditions are right for a tornado to form when a fast moving cold front meets the warm air near the earth's surface. The air masses collide and the result can be violent storm systems. While conditions might be favorable for a tornado to occur, tornadoes are unpredictable, allowing people in the area only ten minutes to prepare or hitting without any warning at all. *(Tornadoes can be researched on the Internet with many pictures that can be downloaded for use during the service.)*

In much the same way, the storms in our lives occur when our daily routines collide with the powerful and fast-moving circumstances that create the conditions for a storm. The scripture gives us insight on how to prepare and survive those storms. The scripture tells us not to worry about anything, to be prayerful, and to give thanks in all things—then the peace of God will be evident in our lives. So let's look at this three-step approach.

Body

I. We need a foundation.
("Do not worry about anything.")

The text reminds us not to worry about anything. Easier said than done. Worry or anxiety is produced by lack of control over the situation at hand. Do you know why tornadoes are the deadliest storms? It is because they cannot be predicted. A tornado can turn and twist in any direction. If you don't have a solid foundation on which to hold, you are not going to be able to trust. Worry comes from a lack of foundation. In the video clip from *Twister,* Bill (Bill Paxton) tells Jo (Helen Hunt) to hold on to something as the tornado comes over them while they are under the bridge. What is our foundation? What do you hold on to?

II. We need to be prepared.
("by prayer and supplication")

People who live in Tornado Alley (Texas, Oklahoma, Kansas, Nebraska, Iowa, and Missouri) know about getting ready for tornado season. Their underground storm shelters are stocked and equipped. The Christian's equivalent to stocking up the storm shelter is being in constant conversation with God. This conversation takes place not only during the storm but also before the storm comes. The apostle's words are "prayerful in everything." The New Testament tells us to "ask God" (twenty times); speaks about prayer (thirty-one times); and uses the word *pray* (sixty-seven times). Prayer is our foundation.

III. We need to embrace life.
("with thanksgiving")

People who live in tornado-prone regions of the world do not stop living when the prime tornado season approaches. They go to work, have children, and enjoy the outdoors. While storms may come, the cycle of life continues. If you put your trust in God, and are living a life of preparedness, you know that you can survive anything.

The apostle is talking about an attitude of thankfulness that is part of the daily life cycle of those prepared for the storm. The language is very important because we are not thankful for everything. I am not thankful when a loved one dies. I am not thankful when children are murdered in school. I am not thankful when a friend loses a job. But I am thankful that in the storm of any circumstance, I am never alone. I am thankful that God knows what the future holds. I am thankful that God wants only the best for my life. Do you see the difference?

IV. Got peace?
("The peace of God, which surpasses all understanding, will guard your hearts and minds in Christ Jesus.")

Peace comes to those who trust in the Lord, who pray for preparation and continue to claim each day in thankfulness.

When Hurricane Andrew roared through Florida, a news report told an extraordinary story. It seemed that a whole neighborhood was demolished. The images from the news reminded one of a war zone. Everything was destroyed, except one thing. In the middle of what used to be someone's home was a table with a small goldfish bowl that remained standing in the middle of this destruction. The goldfish was swimming along contentedly and was oblivious to the miracle of its survival.

I think the peace of God that is described in Philippians is like that goldfish. The storm around us can rage, but the real peace comes from deep inside our spirits. We can survive the storm!

NOTES_____

_____

_____

_____

_____

_____

_____

_____

_____

_____

_____

_____

_____

_____

_____

_____

_____

_____

_____

_____

_____

_____

_____

_____

_____

_____

_____

_____

_____

_____

_____

_____

What's Possessing You?

Ordinary Time

(10 min.) Pastor or WL: Introduction to the service
      1. "Arise and Sing" (Ray) C&W, 13

WL: Lead Call to Worship.
      2. "I Am Not My Own" (Nystrom) SB#6, 491
      3. "I'm So Glad" (unknown) SB#6, 495

WL: Read the Invocation during the introduction to the next song.
      4. "Only by Grace" (Gustafson) C&W, 140

Pastor or WL: Conclude the song with a prayer, then ask the ushers to receive the offering.

Solo: "I Want Jesus to Walk with Me" (Spiritual) UMH, 521

(30 min.) Pastor: Sermon, first tell or read the scripture (Luke 8:26-39) and talk about possessions. *(Display "What's Possessing You?")*

    I. Materialism. Show clip from *Indiana Jones and the Last Crusade* (Paramount Pictures)
    Description: Indiana Jones just used the chalice to heal his father's bullet wound.
    Start Time: 1:56:46
    Start Cue: Indiana: "Dad, get to your feet."
    End Time: 1:58:36
    End Cue: Professor Jones: "Indiana, let it go!"

    II. Addictions. Play the song "Remember Your Chains" by Steven Curtis Chapman, from *Heaven in the Real World* (Sparrow Records) with coordinated pictures. *(See song script.)*
    III. Pride: Skit, *Pretty Proud of It*
    IV. Lifestyles: Tie up a person with yarn.

(5 min.) Pastor: Lead congregational prayer time. Give everyone the opportunity to write on a piece of paper: "What is possessing you?"

(10 min.) Response to the Word: People can come forward to drop their slips of paper into a container. Set the papers on fire. Play reflective music during this time. The pastor concludes by cutting loose the person who is tied up. *(See sermon notes.)*

PT: Lead the closing song.
      5. "He Whom the Son Sets Free" (Nystrom) SB#6, 483

Pastor or WL: Benediction

Music Sources: *Praise Worship Songbook #6* (Integrity); *Praise Hymns and Choruses (4th ed)* (Maranatha); *Songs for Praise & Worship* (Word); *The United Methodist Hymnal* (UMPH)

INTRODUCTION TO THE SERVICE

What is in control of your life? I don't know what is keeping you enslaved, but when you leave, you can leave it behind because Christ has broken your bondage.

CALL TO WORSHIP

L: We want to see Jesus.

P: Yes, but in the presence of the Holy One our sin is exposed.

L: We need Jesus.

P: Yes, we need Jesus to set us free from our sin.

INVOCATION

Jesus, Son of the High God, we live in the bondage of sin, which has separated us from your love. We cry out to be made whole. You hear our cry and your grace meets us at our need. Only by grace can we enter into your presence. Amen.

Song Script: *(Suggested pictures/slides to be displayed during the song.)*

Verse 1: A person's hands on prison bars/metal chains

Chorus: A person in a prison cell/empty prison cell/cocaine/metal chains/black slide

Verse 2: Hungry child (children)/unemployed/a person in thought/a person reading the Bible in prison

Chorus: A person in a prison cell/empty prison cell/metal chains/open door

Verse 3: Open door with bright light shining through

Chorus: Picture of metal chains/words that depict our chains (e.g., drugs, money, work, relationships)

Verse 4: Metal chains/black slide/three crosses

Sermon Skit: Improvise a skit concerning issues about pride that are current in your community, or consider purchasing *Pretty Proud of It* by Dave McClellan.

(Cross Point Scripts #12410; see introduction for resource.)

Skit Synopsis *(Three people and a narrator)*

This sketch takes a sort of backdoor look at pride. We'd all say that pride is bad and that we certainly don't want to be known as proud people. In fact, we're so confident that we don't have a problem with pride that we might even

be proud of it. That's the subtlety of pride. It often lurks undetected.

(The first person is proud of his or her own achievements and boasts of all accomplishments. The second person is critical of anyone who accomplishes more than he or she does. The third person appears to be tolerant but is, in fact, proud of being politically correct. The narrator gives an analysis of each person's pride after he or she has spoken.)

BENEDICTION #1: See sermon notes.

BENEDICTION #2:

Just as Jesus sent the man home that had been set free, I send you forth with the same words, "Go home and tell everything God is doing in you." Hallelujah, Amen.

ALTAR

A burlap cloth covers the altar. In the center is a black, iron candelabra draped with hemp-type rope. Double iron candleholders are on either side. Silk greenery is used for filler. The Bible is placed in the center front to represent the One who sets us free from bondage. A large metal chain and rope are draped on the altar to represent our bondage. The metal bucket on the floor in front of the altar will hold the pieces of paper (what's possessing you?) that will be collected and burned.

OPTIONS

Music 🎵

"Lord, I Lift Your Name on High" (Founds) *Cokesbury Chorus Book* (Abingdon Press)

"He Will Deliver Me" (Batstone) *Praise Hymns & Choruses (4th ed.)* (Maranatha)

"Change My Heart, O God" (Espinosa) *Cokesbury Chorus Book* (Abingdon Press)

"Create in Me a Clean Heart" (unknown) *Praise Hymns & Choruses (4th ed.)* (Maranatha)

"I Come to the Cross" (Somma/Batstone) *Praise Hymns & Choruses* (Maranatha)

"Let the Walls Fall Down" (Batstone & Barbour) *Praise Hymns & Choruses* (Maranatha)

"Spirit Song" (Wimber) *Cokesbury Chorus Book* (Abingdon Press)

"People Need the Lord" (Nelson/McHugh) *Cokesbury Chorus Book* (Abingdon Press)

Recordings

"Busy Man" as performed by Steven Curtis Chapman, from *For The Sake Of The Call* (Sparrow Records)

"More to This Life" as performed by Steven Curtis Chapman, from *More To This Life* (Sparrow Records)

"Things of This Word" as performed by D.C. Talk, from *Nu Thang* (Forefront Records)

Drama

The Basement by Dave McClellan (Cross Point Script #12230; see introduction.)

(Husband and wife, five to six minutes)

Purpose: We all try to hang on to things from the past. It's the only way we know to preserve the moments that we're sure are passing too quickly. Unfortunately, this preservation of our past often inhibits our generosity in meeting the needs of others. We must learn, as the scriptures say, that "life does not consist in the abundance of possessions."

SERMON

Idea Generator

At first glance one might think that a story about demon possession would have no relevance to the contemporary worship setting. However, the key to applying this text to your congregation starts with applying it to your own life. What possesses you? As a time of reflection, think a moment on what is holding you back. What is chaining you down? As pastors, we don't like to think that we allow ourselves to be chained or bound by anything. But pastors often feel overwhelming congregational demands and expectations that keep them from fulfilling their true calling as pastors. We start to define ourselves by these expectations. Instead of living in freedom as a child of God, we are trapped in bondage by the expectations of those around us. Instead of living in the light of God's love, we live in a dark, dead place. Sounds a bit like the living conditions of the Gerasene demoniac. What is possessing you?

Sermon Note: This is a wonderful sermon to deliver in segmented form using a variety of media and experiential opportunities. This sermon is divided into four segments and uses an outline for people to take home.

Introduction

This is an excellent scripture for a storyteller preacher to paraphrase. However, if you would like to read the scripture, consider using *THE MESSAGE* by Eugene Peterson.

Body

I. Materialism

In one of my seminary classes, the professor was asked what he considered to be the greatest sin. His reply was, "In this country, consumerism." We are a nation built on profit and the right to make money and buy things. Isn't that the American Dream?

I believe the professor really did name America's greatest sin. Material things, possessions, status symbols are often at the heart of our deepest spiritual problems. In fact, the very word *possession* means something that has control or influence over something else. Is it not ironic that the things we seek to possess eventually could consume or perhaps even destroy us? There is a clip from the movie *Indiana Jones and the Last Crusade*, which offers a classic example of this extreme. *(See script.)*

II. Addictions

Perhaps the most baffling and disheartening experience in life is to be caught in the grips of something that binds you and with which you have no control. No one chooses to be addicted. It is only an act of grace by God that can free you from the addiction.

Anyone who watches evening television magazine shows is able to identify the epidemic proportions of these societal ills: alcoholism, drug abuse, gambling, and sexual addictions. But there are life dependencies we are less able and willing to identify: the executive who goes to work early and stays late to avoid the reality of his failing marriage; the woman looking for love who finds herself continually involved in destructive relationships; the man who seeks approval from the authority figures in his life because his self-esteem is based on other's opinions.

Jesus often asked people if they wanted to be made whole. It seems like a strange question, but for those who find themselves in the grip of addiction it is an important question. The chains of addiction can only be broken when people admit their powerlessness over the addiction. While the person wants to be well, the addict cannot do it on his or her own terms. Only by admitting their powerlessness to make themselves well, can those addicted begin the journey to wholeness. An illustration of this is found in the song "Remember Your Chains" by Steven Curtis Chapman. *(See script.)*

III. Pride

"Pride goes before destruction, and a haughty spirit before a fall" (Prov. 16:18). This famous proverb is often quoted in church—with pride, I might add. It is easy to point to the pride we take in our accomplishments. We are a nation built on a sense of pride. We cheer our own team in sports events; we want our country's team to win Olympic gold. Being first in any competition becomes an all-consuming goal for the players and fans. "We're number one" becomes the battle cry. Woe to the winning football coach who does not meet the expectation of the fans the year following the national championship season.

Perhaps the greatest danger of all to Christians is religious pride. We look down on others' religious experiences because they are not like ours. If we stand under the banner of conservatism, we take great pride in judging who is in and who is out. If we stand under the banner of liberalism, we take great pride in deciding who is wrong and who is right. Such prideful discussions have led to passionate debate over Jesus' political affiliation and "where he would be if he came back right now." *(See script for dramatic example.)*

IV. Lifestyle

(Note that the preacher uses yarn to tie up someone during this segment as the particulars of your congregation's lifestyle are examined. Wrap the volunteer with yarn as you say the word "right.")

The demoniac's lifestyle was not what we would aspire to for ourselves. And yet, our lifestyles can be just as destructive and unfulfilling. Having the *right* car, belonging to the *right*

country club, sending our children to the *right* private school can sometimes drive us *right* up the wall in our house in the *right* neighborhood. This *right* kind of life can literally tie us up in knots. Having nice things and aspiring to have nice things is not evil, but when these things become a never-ending status treadmill, our faith journeys remain stationary. Our desire and need to maintain a certain lifestyle can immobilize us. *(At this point, the volunteer would be tied with yarn so that bondage is visually illustrated.)*

Conclusion

Just as the demoniac received healing, you may also experience healing by leaving whatever is possessing you. Sometimes it takes a ritual to really claim the healing power of God. Take a few minutes and write down whatever is possessing you. Then as you feel led, come forward and drop your paper into the container. *(Set the papers in the container on fire. Place something under the container to protect the floor from the heat and be sure that smoke alarms will not go off.)*

Benediction #1:

(As you proclaim the benediction, cut the yarn that is binding the volunteer.) Jesus has broken your bondage. The chains that have held you are broken. You are free!

NOTES _____

_____

_____

_____

_____

_____

_____

_____

_____

_____

Gourmet Dining

All Saints Sunday

Prelude: Taped music (chant, mystical, meditative)

(10 min.)   **Pastor:** Welcome the people and read the Invitation that each person received when entering the service.

WL: Lead unison Invocation.
1. "We Celebrate" (Till/Davenport) SFPW, 162
2. "People of God" (Watson) SFPW, 139
3. "Come Into the King's Chambers" (Gardner) SFPW, 24

Pastor or WL: Read the names of those in the congregation who have died the past year, as a candle on the altar is lighted for each one. Play soft background music.

(15 min.)   **Pastor or WL:** Read prayer.
4. "Come to the Table" (Cloninger/Nystrom) SB#6, 471

Interpretive Dance: Use "Come Expecting Jesus" (Chisum, Gordon) from *Because We Believe* by John Chisum as the music for the dance. *(Bread and juice should be brought to the altar by the dancers.)*

WL: Read or tell the scripture lesson (John 6:27-34).
5. "Jehovah to Me" (Keesecker) SFPW, 231

(15 min.)   **Pastor:** Sermon

(10 min.)   **Communion:** As communion is served, play the same type music that was used for the prelude.

Pastor: Offer a time of commitment.

PT: Lead closing songs.
6. "Holy Ground" (Beatty) SFPW, 85
7. "Holy Ground" (Davis) SFPW, 86

Pastor: Benediction

Music Sources: *Praise Worship Songbook #6* (Integrity); *Songs for Praise & Worship* (Word)

INVITATION

(Type inside a scroll with old English font. Hand out to each worshiper upon entering.)

𝔍𝔢𝔰𝔲𝔰 𝔠𝔥𝔯𝔦𝔰𝔱 𝔬𝔲𝔯 𝔏𝔬𝔯𝔡 𝔯𝔢𝔮𝔲𝔢𝔰𝔱𝔰 𝔱𝔥𝔢
honor of your presence
at a formal meal given for
all God's people
on the ( ) day of the ( ) month
in the Year of our Lord, Two Thousand.

INVOCATION

Jesus Christ our Lord, we are overwhelmed by your extravagant hospitality. You prepare before us a gracious table where all may come in equality and love. Even though we appear to be separated from those in the faith who have gone before us, we are bound together when we come to your table. We are honored to accept your invitation. Amen.

PRAYER

Eternal God, we come into your presence in unity with all our loved ones who have gone before us. For a season we may grieve, but you tell us that we will not be left comfortless and forsaken. You have prepared a place for our loved ones and for us. You have promised us that as you were raised from the dead, we shall be raised also. This is our hope that we will be reunited with one another in your everlasting kingdom. Amen.

COMMUNION LITURGY

From *The United Methodist Book of Worship* (All Saints), p. 74. *(Other worship resources for All Saints Day could also be used.)*

BENEDICTION

You have feasted at the Lord's table. Now you are invited to go into the world to extend God's invitation to all people. Hallelujah, Amen!

ALTAR

The altar is extended with a table on either side. White lace cloths are used on the center altar and on both tables. On the center altar place one white candle for each church mem-ber who has died in the past year. One central candle is lighted for those not named, but remembered. A symbolic loaf of communion bread is in the center front of the altar, representing our communion with all the saints of the church. Each side table is adorned with silver candelabra, communion bread on a silver tray, and communion wine in a silver goblet. There is also a silver bowl holding grapes on each table. Large ferns are placed at the end of both tables. The setting should be as formal as possible.

OPTIONS

Music ♫

"By Your Blood" (Gustafson/Nystrom) *Come & Worship* (Integrity)

"In Remembrance" (Courtney/Red) *The Celebration Hymnal* (Word/Integrity)

"Let Us Break Bread Together" (Traditional) *The United Methodist Hymnal* (UMPH)

"Remember Me" (Gustafson/Nystrom) *Come & Worship* (Integrity)

"We Remember You" (Dearman) *Songs for Praise & Worship* (Word)

"You Who Are Thirsty" (Ross) *Songs for Praise & Worship* (Word)

SERMON

Idea Generator

I am a single person and meals at my house are usually eaten in front of the television or the computer. During the day, I grab something in the church kitchen or call in an order somewhere so that I can get back to my desk. I used to think I did this because I didn't have a spouse or children with whom to enjoy a long leisurely meal. But in conversation with my friends who have spouses and/or children, I find that this is everybody's lifestyle. Families rarely eat meals together and they almost certainly do not make it a regular practice to eat meals on the family's best china and silver.

There is a bonding that occurs when we share bread with someone else. Yet, for most of us that experience has become another task to check off our list. The people gathered for communion may have come to the worship space having rushed through a meal they shared together so they could get to worship on time. When they leave, they should be assured of Jesus' communion grace. Communion grace cannot be rushed or received miserly. God's love is extravagant.

Sermon Starter

Pastor: (*The preacher rushes to the front with a fast-food take-out bag.*) Well, it's time for communion. (*Holds the bag up for the congregation to see.*) Are you ready? I brought the communion elements. Let's get this over with. (*Places the bag on the altar.*)

Introduction

When was the last time you sat down for a long, leisurely meal? Was the table set with beautiful china, crystal, and silver? Were there candles and flowers adorning the table? If this were the case and the meal was exquisitely prepared, you probably felt overwhelmed by your environment and your host's graciousness.

Our table today is the Lord's Table. It is set for you to receive the graciousness of your host, Jesus.

Body

Last week, I had dinner with a good friend. We were both celebrating recent birthdays. We decided to go to the best restaurant in town where we enjoyed a three-hour dining experience. The food was wonderfully prepared. The table was set beautifully. There was lovely music. All the elements added pleasure to our dining and made for a pleasurable evening. But the key element to our enjoyment was each other's company.

Jesus told his disciples that he was the bread of life, that whoever comes to him will never be hungry. Jesus wants to be our dining companion. He wants to provide us with the real bread. Jesus is the bread of life that will sustain and empower us for our journey.

But how often do we fill up on fast food that leaves us feeling empty and unsatisfied? (*Lift up the fast-food bag.*) We substitute a dining experience with Jesus with a drive-through, fat-loaded junk meal of fast food. No wonder we feel stressed. No wonder we feel burned out. No wonder we feel empty.

Conclusion

We are spiritually hungry because we look to the wrong source for our spiritual nourishment. Jesus is the Bread of Life. On this day of celebration for All Saints, Jesus is our host and we are surrounded by a multitude of fellow diners.

We can look around and see that we are a part of a community of faith where everyone is welcome at Jesus' table. But our table includes many others that are not physically present. There is a multitude we cannot see with our eyes. Those loved ones that have died in the faith also take their place with us at this table. There is a term we use to describe this gathering. It is called the Communion of Saints.

We are a part of the Communion of Saints because Jesus offers grace to begin our lives anew in relationship with him. We are one community gathered around the table of our gracious host, Jesus. Jesus has not invited us to a fast-food meal; he has invited us to be his guests with the best he can offer us—Living Bread. We need never be hungry again. You are invited to the table of Jesus. Come and be fed.

NOTES

_____

_____

_____

_____

_____

_____

_____

_____

_____

_____

Touched by an Angel

First Sunday of Advent

(10 min.)   **Pastor:** Welcome/announcements. Begin the service with a prayer.

PT enter from the back singing "O Come, O Come, Emmanuel" (UMH, 211). Begin as an unaccompanied solo and add one voice with each new phrase, repeating the refrain for the congregation to join in. Each **PT** member should carry an item to place on the altar or a candle to put in the Advent wreath.

WL: Lead Call to Worship
1. "Jesus, Come/Emmanuel" (Townley) CC, 23

Lighting the Advent Candle (*Use a reading of your choice.*)
2. "Holy Baby, Holy Child" (Hurst) (See end of script.)
3. "Like a Rose in Winter" (Hanson/Murakami) CC, 24
4. "Angels, from the Realms of Glory" (Montgomery/Smart) TCH, 259
5. "Worthy, You Are Worthy" (Moen) TCH, 260

(10 min.)   **Pastor:** Lead congregational prayer time.

PT: Sing the scripture (Luke 1:26-38).
6. "To a Maid Engaged to Joseph" (Grindal/Edwards) UMH, 215
(This can be sung by three singers: Narrator, Gabriel, and Mary.)

(20 min.)   **Pastor:** Sermon
  I. God Be with You
 II. No Fear
III. Nothing Is Impossible

(10 min.)   **Time of Reflection and Offering:** Interpretive dance or a person signing to "Breath of Heaven" (Eaton/Grant), Age to Age Music, 1992

Time of Commitment
7. "Of the Father's Love Begotten" (Traditional) TCH, 240
*(**PT** only, sing unaccompanied or with flute/oboe accompaniment. Begin as a solo and add voices.)*

Pastor: Lead Benediction.

Music Sources: *Come Celebrate!* (Abingdon Press); *The Celebration Hymnal* (Word/Integrity); *The United Methodist Hymnal* (UMPH)

CALL TO WORSHIP

L: O come, O come, Emmanuel.

P: Can we ask God to come into our ordinary lives?

L: O come, O come, Emmanuel.

P: Will we recognize God in the busyness of this season?

L: O come, O come, Emmanuel.

P: Teach us to be prepared to hear the extraordinary.

All: O come, O come, Emmanuel.

BENEDICTION ("Repeat after me.")

God is with us. We have nothing to fear. The impossible is now possible. Hallelujah, Amen!

Holy Baby, Holy Child

LYNN S. HURST

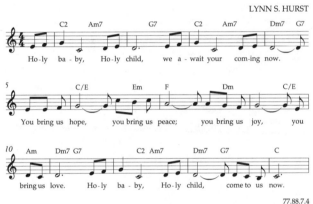

77.88.7.4

© 2000 Abingdon Press

ALTAR

A small table covered with a white cloth is placed in front of the altar. Purple fabric is draped from the center music stand, onto the altar, and over the small table onto the floor. An off-white and gold table runner is placed on either side of the altar. A large gold angel frame with a three-wick candle is placed in the center. Poinsettias are placed on either side. The Advent wreath is on the small table in front of the altar. *(The angel candleholder, poinsettias, and Advent wreath candles can be brought in during the processional by the Praise Team.)*

OPTIONS

Music

"Arise, Shine" (Urspringer/Robinson) *The Celebration Hymnal* (Word/Integrity)

"Arise, Shine" (Smith) *Cokesbury Chorus Book* (Abingdon Press)

"Help Me Wait" (Townley) *Come Celebrate!* (Abingdon Press)

"I Extol You" (Randolph) *The Celebration Hymnal* (Word/Integrity)

"We Bow Down" (Paris) *Songs for Praise & Worship* (Word)

Recordings

"Celebrate the Gift" (Paris) as performed by Twila Paris, from the Christmas CD, *Celebrate the Gift* (Star Song Records)

SERMON

Idea Generator

For the pastor, the Advent season has unique challenges. While church attendance has a tendency to climb during this time of year, many folks are burned out by the time Christmas actually arrives. Often, there is no concept of preparing one's heart for the Christ Child. Everyone is too busy preparing his or her homes and schedules. Unfortunately, the church tends to add pressure during this season.

This is the first in a series of Advent sermons looking at how God may speak to us and how God comes into our busy lives to be with us. Statistics tell us that depression is high during this season. People want to be able to know that God cares for them. The pastor has the word of hope. How can we be messengers of God's hope without adding more pressure to the season?

Introduction

I like to think how surprised Hollywood has been by the popularity of the television show, *Touched by an Angel.* The show's simple theme each week is "God loves you." It seems this has touched the heart of the viewing public. This new trend has not gone unnoticed by the rest of the media. Books about angels are among the best-sellers and everyone knows that angels are hot collectibles. There are even angel web sites. Why all this fuss about angels?

Angels are spiritual beings created by God. In scripture they protect people, offer encouragement, give guidance, bring punishment, patrol the earth, fight forces of evil, and offer continuous praise to God. Those of us reading scripture may view the appearance of an angel as unusual. But to the writers of scripture, the appearance of an angel was more than just a visit by a supernatural being. The word *angel* means messenger. A visit by an angel meant that God had a message for the one that was being visited.

Maybe this is the place in which our heart is touched by all this fascination with angels. We are all seeking a message from God. Listen to the message that Mary receives from God, and you will hear a message for our time.

Body

I. God Is with You (vv. 26-28)

The angel told Mary that God was with her. How do we know God is with us? Do we know based on our outward circumstances? If we are healthy, wealthy, and wise does that mean that God is with us? NO. Mary would not have been considered someone who was a powerful, influential person. Based on her outward circumstances, she was a poor teenage girl in a backward region of the world.

While I was in seminary, I helped deliver meals to elderly people in a poor section of town. One lady to whom I delivered food always praised God for her blessings and God's presence with her. I would look around her meager apartment and then I would look at her. She was blind and poor. And yet, she knew God was with her. It wasn't the outward circumstances.

Do we know God is with us based on how we feel? NO. I have heard people say many times, "I don't feel like a Christian." It is true that sometimes we don't feel like Christians. Sometimes I am physically sick and I don't feel like a Christian. I'm cranky and self-centered at those times. But God's presence is not dependent on my feelings. There was a time when John Wesley did not feel like he had faith and he was told: "Preach faith till you have it; and then because you have it you will preach faith." His faith was not dependent on how he felt. Do we know God is with us based on our feelings? NO.

How do we know God is with us? God is with us based on a promise. God is with us because God chooses to be with us, not because we decide God is with us. The angel told Mary that God was with her and she believed. Jesus assures the disciples and those who follow him today: "Surely I am with you always, to the very end of the age" (Matt. 28:20 NIV). Believe because God has told you.

II. No Fear (vv. 29-33)

In every story about a mortal's encounter with an angel, the conversation usually includes the words, "Do not fear" or "Do not be afraid." I wonder why the angel would bring this message to Mary? Perhaps it is because this encounter with God's messenger brings an uncertainty about Mary's future.

What causes fear? It is usually uncertainty about something or some situation. When a child cries out in the night for Mommy or Daddy because of the belief that there is a monster under the bed, there is fear. What kind of monster is under our bed?

But as Mary discovered, she did not have to fear because God had a plan for her life. God has a plan for each one of us so we do not have to fear. God's plan for our lives was not acted out in some otherworldly sphere. God's plan included a divine action. God was to become like one of us. If God will be with us, what do we have to fear?

III. Nothing Is Impossible (vv. 34-38)

Mary had a natural question for the messenger—"How can this be?" The angel's response to Mary reminds the listener that God's message for each one of us is the same: "What is impossible for mortals is possible for God." But, what made the impossible possible? The key for everyone seeking to hear God's message is that Mary *chose* to become a part of God's plan for her life and for all of humanity. She was willing to become a cocreator with God, and through her willingness the impossible was made possible.

God waits for our response to the message. Will we respond out of a superficial understanding of God's presence? Will we respond out of fear of the future? If we do, we will probably miss the impossible made possible. Or will we respond as Mary did: "Let it be with me according to your will." From this response, God's plan for humanity became a reality. God came to be with us, to die for us, and to live that we might live.

How will YOU respond to the message?

Friends

2nd Sunday of Advent, Communion

(15 min.) **PT** enters to the theme music of the T.V. sitcom *Friends*. They should depict the mood of the service by waving to friends.

WL: Lead Call to Worship
1. "Love Has Come!" (Bible) TCH, 256
2. "Joyful, Joyful, We Adore You" (Text: Johnson) TCH, 271
3. "Let's Worship and Adore Him" (Traditional) TCH, 247

Lighting the Advent Candles *(Use a reading of your choice.)*
4. "Holy Baby, Holy Child" (Hurst) *(See page 31.)*

WL: Read prayer as the introduction to the next song.
5. "Behold, What Manner of Love" (VanTine) SFPW, 48
6. "Let There Be Praise" (Tunney) SFPW, 250
7. "He Is Exalted" (Paris) SFPW, 66

(25 min.) **Pastor:** Scripture and sermon
I. Friends Rejoice
II. Friends Care
   (Lead congregational prayer time.)
III. Friends Reflect

(10 min.) **Communion:** While communion is served, play "You've Got a Friend" by Carol King (Screen Gems/Columbia Music, 1971). Offerings may be brought forward during communion.

Time of Commitment
8. "Good Christian Friends, Rejoice" stanzas 2, 3
(Trans: Neale) CC, 27

Pastor: Benediction

Music Sources: *The Celebration Hymnal* (Word/Integrity); *Songs for Praise & Worship* (Word); *Come Celebrate!* (Abingdon Press)

CALL TO WORSHIP

L: Some days, Lord, I want to laugh and sing. My heart is bursting with good news and I need to tell my best friend.

P: God, you delight in the praise of your people. You rejoice with us and you send us best friends to dance with us and share our good news.

L: And then there are the other days, God. The days I need someone to care and be my comfort. Those are the days I need God with some skin on.

P: God you hear our cries and cry with us. Through the words of our family, the kindness of a stranger or the touch of a child, we experience care and comfort on those difficult days.

L: In your son, Jesus, we experience love realized. Your people are a reflection of God's love.

P: Because you first loved us, we can love as Friends of God.

PRAYER

"This is my commandment, that you love one another as I have loved you. No one has greater love than this, to lay down one's life for one's friends. You are my friends if you do what I command you. I do not call you servants any longer, because the servant does not know what the master is doing; but I have called you friends, because I have made known to you everything that I have heard from my Father" (John 15:12-15). Help us, Lord, to so love one another that your love may be reflected to our friends. Amen.

PRAYER OF CONSECRATION

One of God's first desires for humanity was companionship. Jesus came to us as a baby to be our companion. While on earth, he called twelve to be his companions on his journey to the cross. Together they traveled, ministered, and broke bread. On the night before he died, Jesus gathered with his friends to share a meal and to bind the community of faith together. He took bread, gave thanks to God, broke the bread, gave it to his friends and said, "Take, eat, this is my body which is given for you." Then he took the cup, gave thanks to God, gave it to his friends and said, "Drink from this, all of you, this is my blood poured out for you. Do this in remembrance of me." And so, in remembrance of your loving actions, pour out your Holy Spirit on this bread and wine and make it be for us the body and blood of Christ, that we may be Christ's body and friend for the world. By your Spirit, make us one in Christ, one with each other, and one in ministry to the entire world, until Christ comes in final victory and we feast together as friends at his heavenly table. Amen.

BENEDICTION

Now we are prepared to hear God through the extraordinary and through friends. Help us as we continue to prepare our hearts to receive your Son. Hallelujah, Amen!

ALTAR

The altar is the same as the first week of Advent with these additions: a small manger is placed on the right side of the altar and the communion elements are on the left side.

OPTIONS

Music

"Come and Praise Him, Royal Priesthood" (Carter) *Songs for Praise & Worship* (Word)

"Emmanuel" (McGee) *Songs for Praise & Worship* (Word)

"I Will Come and Bow Down" (Nystrom) *Songs for Praise & Worship* (Word)

"I Extol You" (Randolph) *Songs for Praise & Worship* (Word)

"Isn't He?" (Wimber) *Songs for Praise & Worship* (Word)

"Jesus Come/Emmanuel" (Townley/McGee) *Come Celebrate!* (Abingdon Press)

"Jesus, Name Above All Names" (Hearn) *Songs for Praise & Worship* (Word)

"We Bow Down" (Paris) *Songs for Praise & Worship* (Word)

Recordings

"Sent By the Father" (Boltz/Millikan) performed by Ray Boltz on *A Christmas Album* (Ray Boltz Music)

"The Season of Love" as performed by 4 Him, from the album, *The Season of Love* (Benson Records)

SERMON

Idea Generator

In this second week of Advent, we again focus on how God speaks to us. If an angel came to us and gave us a direct message from God we would know God's plan for our life. However, the scripture text that we focus on this Sunday reminds us that God speaks to us through the ordinary as well as the extraordinary.

The community of faith is challenged to become listeners as we help our brothers and sisters discern God's will. As a spiritual exercise this week, think of those close companions who help you, the pastor, in your discernment process. What characteristics do they possess and how do they reflect God's love to you?

Introduction

Last week we heard the message Mary received from God through a supernatural messenger. Everyone would probably confess that it would be great if God entered our lives in this manner. We would know without a doubt what God's will is for our lives. Right? Well, maybe.

Today's text reminds us that God speaks to us in the seemingly ordinary relationships, ones that can become for us a reflection of God's love. What happened after the angel left Mary? We can only imagine. Mary was an unwed teenage mother. What would happen in our hometown or community? People would whisper and gossip. The pressure on a young girl would be overwhelming. But God had not abandoned Mary. Scripture tells us that she sought the companionship of her cousin Elizabeth, an older, wiser, godly woman. Elizabeth was Mary's wise counsel and she was also pregnant. She could not only sympathize, she could empathize.

God told Adam it was not good for humans to be alone. Perhaps the companionship of another is one of the deepest needs of humanity. In the television show, *Friends,* six people who share in life's ups and downs become a family. Friends are essential in life. The dictionary defines a friend as "one who is personally well known by oneself and for whom one has warm regard or affection." But, I don't think that really defines friendship. I like the defini-

tion a friend cross-stitched and gave to me: "A real friend is one who overlooks your broken down gate and admires the flowers in your windows." What do we learn about how God speaks to us through this scripture of the friendship between Mary and Elizabeth?

Body

I. Friends Rejoice

When something exciting and joyful happens in my life, I want to share it with my best friend. Elizabeth rejoiced with Mary. How different a reaction than the one Mary probably received in her hometown. Elizabeth believed that this was God's miracle and plan for Mary. She believed Mary's story and rejoiced with her.

Elizabeth didn't react with envy that her own child was not the promised Messiah. She reacted in love. In her rejoicing with Mary, she put flesh on God's promise to Mary. She spoke and confirmed God's words.

II. Friends Care

Elizabeth cared about Mary. I can only imagine Elizabeth in her advanced state of pregnancy nurturing Mary in her beginning trimester. When someone has walked the road you are traveling, he or she understands the circumstances in which you find yourself. This person cares and stands beside you. "A friend loves at all times, and kinsfolk are born to share adversity" (Prov. 17:17).

I remember a time in my life when I was going through a deep personal crisis. I was traveling home from a meeting when I had become so distraught I could hardly drive. I immediately called a friend from my cell phone. She prayed with me and told me to come straight to her house. It was late when I got there, but she had put on a pot of coffee. She was prepared to be there for as long as I needed. There were no words she had to offer that made the difference, but through her care and presence I clearly heard God's love for me.

III. Friends Reflect

Like my friend, your friends can reflect God's love. How wonderful for Mary to have Elizabeth's friendship during those difficult months. There were no other visitations by angels, but the message of God's love must have come through very clearly by Elizabeth's presence.

Friends help us by physically reflecting God's love. A friend can become God with skin on. Friends also help us to think clearly by listening to us and reminding us of the truth. One of my colleagues in ministry has a gift for reminding me of my status as a child of God. Whenever I allow the pressures and voices of others to tell me otherwise, she helps me focus on who I really am and on my calling from God. Friends reflect God's love through actions, words, and presence.

Maya Angelou recounts how a friend reflected God's love to her:

> One day the teacher, Frederick Wilkerson, asked me to read to him. I was twenty-four, very erudite, very worldly. He asked that I read from *Lessons in Truth*, a section that ended with these words: "God loves me." I read the piece and closed the book, and teacher said, "Read it again." I pointedly opened the book, and I sarcastically read, "God loves me." He said, "Again." After about the seventh repetition I began to sense that there might be truth in the statement, that there was a possibility that God really did love me. Me, Maya Angelou. I suddenly began to cry at the grandness of it all. I knew that if God loved me, then I could do wonderful things. I could try great things, learn anything, achieve anything. For what could stand against me with God, since one person, any person with God constitutes the majority? (*Wouldn't Take Nothing for My Journey Now* [New York: Random House, 1993], p. 75).

Maya Angelou encountered a friend who opened to her the truth of her relationship with God and God's desire to be in relationship with her.

NOTES

36

What Dreams May Come

3rd Sunday of Advent

(15 min.) **WL and Pastor:** Call to Worship skit, *Sleepless Nights*
1. "Angels We Have Heard on High" (Traditional) PHC, 87
2. "Joy to the World!" (Watts/Handel) TCH, 270
3. "Joyful, Joyful, We Adore You" (Johnson/Beethoven) TCH, 271

WL: Lead Call to Worship.
4. "O Little Town of Bethlehem" (Brooks/Redner) CC, 26
5. "Come and Behold Him" (Chisum/Searcy) SB#9, 722

Lighting the Advent Candles *(Use a reading of your choice.)*
6. "Holy Baby, Holy Child" (Hurst) (See page 31.)
7. "Let's Worship and Adore Him" (Traditional) TCH, 247

(15 min.) **Pastor:** Lead congregational prayer time. Introduce the scripture
video or read the scripture (Matt. 1:18-24).
(See the *Visual Bible,* Visual Fulfillment Services.)

Anthem: "One Small Child" (Meece) GlorySound, 1981

(20 min.) **Pastor:** Sermon
I. Sleepless Nights
II. God Hears the Heart Cry
III. Peace Comes with the Son

(10 min.) **Time of Reflection and Offering**

Anthem or Solo: "A Litany for Advent" (McRae) Choristers Guild, 1991

Time of Commitment
8. "Arise, Shine" (O'Brien/Davis) PHC, 88

Pastor or WL: Benediction

Music Sources: *Praise Hymns & Choruses (4th ed.)* (Maranatha); *The Celebration Hymnal* (Word/Integrity); *Come Celebrate!* (Abingdon Press); *Praise Songbook #9* (Integrity)

Permission is granted to purchaser to copy for local church praise team.

37

CALL TO WORSHIP SKIT: *Sleepless Nights*

WL#1: (*Yawning continuously*)

WL#2: What's the matter with you?

WL#1: I'm so tired. I didn't sleep at all last night, I just tossed and turned. (*Continues complaining until the pastor interrupts.*)

Pastor: Wait, wait! Have you ever felt like that? Today we're going to hear a story about a man who felt the same way, but his sleeplessness opened the possibility for God to speak.

CALL TO WORSHIP

(*Designate two groups for the Call to Worship.*)

L: O come, O come, Emmanuel!
Group 1: We have heard you through the extraordinary.
Group 2: Help us break down the walls of fear.
L: O come, O come, Emmanuel!
Group 1: We have heard you through our friends.
Group 2: Help us be open to a diversity of friendships.
L: O come, O come, Emmanuel!
All: Give us rest in your peace.

BENEDICTION

Be assured that your restless nights have potential to become the enfleshed dreams of God. Go dream! Hallelujah, Amen!

ALTAR

The altar is the same as the second week of Advent with the addition of white tulle on top of the altar to represent dreams. The communion elements are not necessary for this week.

OPTIONS

Music

"Arise, Shine" (Smith) *Cokesbury Chorus Book* (Abingdon Press)
"Arise, Shine" (Urspringer/Robinson) *The Celebration Hymnal* (Word/Integrity)
"Emmanuel" (McGee) *Songs for Praise & Worship* (Word)

"Jesus Come/Emmanuel" (Townley/McGee) *Come Celebrate!* (Abingdon Press)
"Jesus, Name Above All Names" ((Hearn) *Cokesbury Chorus Book* (Abingdon Press)
"Jesus, Your Name" (Chapman/Cloninger) *Praise Hymns & Choruses* (Maranatha)

Recording

"Sent By the Father" as performed by Ray Boltz on *A Christmas Album* (Ray Boltz Music)
"Unto Us" as performed by Sandi Patti, from *Another Time, Another Place* (Word Records)

Movie

L.A. Story (TriStar Pictures)

SERMON

Idea Generator

Whenever I am under a great deal of stress it seems like my sleep patterns are disturbed. I am certain that I am not alone. There are a lot of yawning, bleary-eyed people in our congregations. I don't think it is just that they have stayed up late the night before. Many have some problem on their mind. Some may have a difficult decision that must be made. For all in our congregation who are having restless nights, Joseph's story offers a word of hope. Emmanuel, God with Us, becomes a reality in the middle of the darkest, most hopeless nights. No other message of this season should sound more loudly and clearly. How can we relay the concept of God's presence with us in a visual, experiential worship service?

Introduction

In the movie *L.A. Story*, a man seeking direction for his life was driving down the highway when he encountered a message on one of those changeable highway signs that was directed at him. I laughed because so many people have said to me, "If only God would give me some sort of sign." For this man there was a literal sign telling him what decisions he should make in his life. At some time in our life every one of us wishes that God would make our decision-making process that clear. We want directions, answers, explanations, assurance, and peace. We want a highway sign from God.

The story of Joseph is one of those stories

that would be easy to miss. In the nativity scene, Joseph seems like one of those silent bit players. What we know of Joseph we find in the first few chapters of Matthew and Luke.

Body

I. Sleepless Nights (vv. 18-19)

We've all had them. A circumstance in our life has created a disruption and sleep seems hopeless. We toss and turn. We try to devise a plan that will still our restless hearts. While the facts of Joseph's life are scant, there is no doubt that his dilemma was overwhelming. The woman he was engaged to was pregnant with a child that was not his own. Think of his feelings. We have all experienced similar feelings of betrayal, anger, and hurt. How do we respond to these feelings?

For Joseph, there appeared to be only two choices. Jewish law gave him two options; neither one was very adequate. Joseph could have Mary stoned because she had committed a sin punishable by death. The other option was to divorce Mary privately and have her sent away. Her shame, the shame brought on the community, and on him, would be hidden and perhaps forgotten.

Joseph's decision leaned toward the choice that seemed the most merciful, giving us a clue that he might be a man with a kind heart. But it is painfully obvious that Joseph struggled, and sought the heart and mind of God in his decision-making process. He wanted to do the right thing.

I don't know what keeps you up at night. I don't know the inner struggles with which you are wrestling. Like Joseph, I am sure you want to do what is right. I also know that as in Joseph's case, God hears and engages in the struggle.

II. God Hears the Heart Cry (vv. 20-21)

The text does not say that Joseph was up struggling with his decision, but it is obvious to every one of us that these kinds of decisions make our hearts weary. The expression that always seems to apply to me during those sleepless nights is "my spirit is wounded." Joseph thought there were only two options, but God is not limited by our perceptions and humanly devised plans. God had another option that had not even appeared as a possibility. For Joseph, who was willing to be obedient to God, the healing for his wounded spirit was found in his willingness to engage God's direction. He followed the God option.

III. Peace Comes with the Son (vv. 22-24)

The name that Joseph is instructed to give this child reflects the ultimate plan and desire of God. Emmanuel, God with us, has come to bring us peace for all those nights in which our hearts cry for direction and peace. Like Joseph, as we honestly seek decisions based on mercy, we will be directed to God's option. As we remember from Mary's encounter with the angel, the God option is not limited by human impossibilities.

Even our restless nights can be a moment of truth as Joseph found. Our restless nights may become the enfleshed dreams of God.

NOTES

_____

_____

_____

_____

_____

_____

_____

_____

_____

_____

_____

_____

_____

Close Encounters

4th Sunday of Advent

(5 min.)	**WL:** Call to Worship skit, *Have You Ever Wondered?*
	Interpretive Dance: "I Wonder as I Wander" (American folk carol), solo or recording
(15 min.)	**WL:** Lead Call to Worship.

    1. "How Great Our Joy!" (Traditional) TCH, 269
    2. "Joy to the World!" (Watts/Handel) TCH, 270
    3. "Joyful, Joyful, We Adore You" (Johnson/Beethoven) TCH, 271

Lighting the Advent Candles: *(Use a reading of your choice.)*
    4. "Holy Baby, Holy Child" (Hurst) (See page 31.)
    5. "What Child Is This?" (Dix) TCH, 281

(5 min.) **Pastor:** Lead congregational prayer time.
    6. "Let's Worship and Adore Him" (Traditional) TCH, 247
    7. "I Extol You" (Randolph) TCH, 248

WL: Read scripture (Luke 2:1-20) and lead songs of preparation.
    8. "Hark! the Herald Angels Sing" (Wesley/Mendelssohn) TCH, 247
    9. "Angels We Have Heard on High" (Traditional) TCH, 278

(20 min.) **Pastor:** Sermon

(10 min.) **Living Nativity Scene:** Have a family (with a young child) dressed in costumes come forward to visually depict the nativity scene while special music (your choice) is being performed or a recording played. Project stars on the ceiling or screen again as at the beginning of the service.

Time of Commitment and Offering: People may bring their offerings forward as the **PT** sings.
    10. "At This Time of Giving" (Kendrick) Make Way Music, 1988

Pastor or WL: Benediction

Music Sources: *The Celebration Hymnal* (Word/Integrity)

Living Water

Alternative Lifestyle

Got Peace?

Photography by Lynn Hurst

What's Possessing You?

Gourmet Dining

Touched by an Angel

Friends

What Dreams May Come/Close Encounters

A Chosen and Marked People

The Mirror of Love

A New Life in a New Land

Who Is This?

While It Was Still Dark, the Son Had Already Risen

Broken Pieces

Paid In Full

Receiving Our Commission

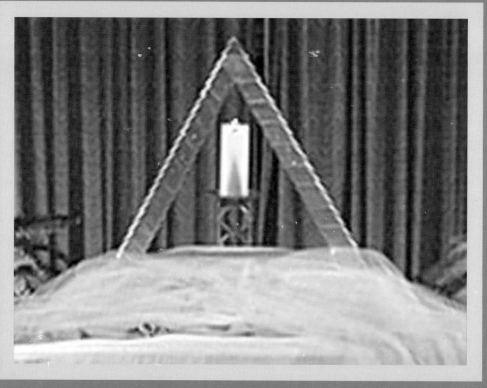

The Jesus files

CALL TO WORSHIP SKIT: *Have You Ever Wondered?*

(The worship space should be as dark as possible. Stars should be projected on the ceiling or on the screen. The theme song from Close Encounters of the Third Kind *begins, or use some other mystical/spacelike music.)*

WL#1: *(Enters slowly while gazing continually at the stars.)*

WL#2: *(Upon entering and seeing WL#1 looking up, WL#2 looks up also.)* Have you ever wondered if there really is something out there?

(Both worship leaders exit. Music for interpretive dance begins, "I Wonder as I Wander.")

CALL TO WORSHIP

L: Have you ever wondered if there really is something out there?
P: Yes, we have wondered.
L: Do you believe we will encounter God out there?
P: No, God will encounter us here.
L: Do you believe God meets us wherever we are?
P: Yes, that is the Good News!

BENEDICTION

I have good news of great joy for everyone. God has come and is with us always. We've had an encounter of the God Kind. Thanks be to God!

ALTAR

The altar is the same as week three of Advent. If possible, have a life-size manger in front of the altar for the living nativity scene. *(See script.)*

OPTIONS

Music ♫ *(Use any Advent/Christmas songs of your choosing.)*

SERMON

Idea Generator

By this point in the Advent season, people are heading into the final countdown for the big event, Christmas. The problem is that Christmas comes to the majority of people as an event to be prepared for and to recover from rather than as the definitive, transformative moment for all human history. Does that seem like a bold statement? The pastor has to understand the inbreaking of the enfleshed God in human history as the source of all we claim to be as Christians. It will be difficult for the pastor who has not taken time to claim this idea to preach this message effectively. What difference does it make that Emmanuel, "God with Us," has come to *be* with us? What difference does it make to the young mother who is stressed out by trying to create the idealized media-driven version of Christmas? What difference does it make to the man who is spending his first Christmas without his wife, who died from cancer three months ago? What difference does it make to the alcoholic who faces a season of cocktail parties and celebrations? What difference does it make to you? If God's appearance to humankind is making a difference, how do you help your congregation visualize this? If God's appearance is not making a difference in your congregation, how do you get back to the basics of our faith?

Introduction

In 1977, *Close Encounters of the Third Kind* was a top box office winner. Even though it has been over twenty years, the movie still has an intriguing hold on us. The tagline of the movie, "We are not alone," could be a creed for the community of faith. As a society we ask the question, "Are we alone?" It is not just a question concerning humankind's place in the galaxy. It is the essential spiritual question for all of us. Are we alone? Is there something or someone out there in the dark, vast universe?

Several years ago, a popular song included these words in the chorus: "God is watching us, from a distance" ("From a Distance," Julie Gold Music Publishing/Wing and Will Publishing, Inc.).

Over the weeks of Advent, we have explored together in a variety of ways how God comes to be with us. Now we have come to the moment in the season in which we affirm we are not alone. God is with us. But God is not with us as a distant entity in the dark, vast universe. God is with us in this moment and place.

Read Luke 2:8-11 at this point in the sermon.

Body

I. Good News

We have good news. That is what the heavenly messengers said to ordinary working people on a hill in Bethlehem. We have all had the experience of someone saying to us, "I have good news and bad news." Usually the news is bad, but the person has to soften the blow with the good news side of the bad news.

God has unequivocal good news. We are not waiting for the other shoe to drop. The Good News is not conditional and it is cause for great joy. When was the last time you heard "good news of great joy"? All too often, Christians are guilty of proclaiming God's judgment rather than the Good News. God's message to the hardworking shepherds did not contain one iota of judgment. It was a proclamation of God's presence. There was a new baby who had come so that we might believe and be in relationship with the God who created the universe. That is Good News! We are not alone.

II. Check It Out

The shepherds not only heard the Good News, they sought to engage the Good News. Hey, let's check this out. If Good News is here, I want to experience the Good News. Notice what the shepherds didn't do. They didn't discuss and vote on the Good News. The shepherds didn't form a task force/committee to investigate and bring a report back about the Good News. The shepherds checked it out themselves immediately. If Good News has come, let's not waste time!

III. Christmas Has Come to You

After engaging the Good News, the shepherds became witnesses and received the Good News personally. They no longer had to rely on a message from a heavenly host. The Good News has come to you. God is with us. We are not alone. God has not waited for you to come to church to experience the Good News. God has come to you right where you are in this moment and time. God has come to your workplace, home, school, community, world, and universe. In the lingo of the culture, encounters of the third kind are physical contacts with extraterrestrials. Encounters of the God Kind are physical contacts with the Creator God. But we don't have to try to bridge the gap and make the contact. God has made contact with us. God visited planet earth as a human so that God, the divine, can be in relationship with us everyday of our lives. That is Good News! We are not alone!

NOTES_____

_____

_____

_____

_____

_____

_____

_____

_____

_____

_____

_____

_____

_____

_____

_____

_____

A Chosen and Marked People

Reaffirmation of Baptism

(10 min.) As people arrive, play recorded music that is reflective in mood and with the sounds of water in the background (e.g., "Majestic Praise" by Dino). If you are using a water fountain *(see altar),* have it turned on as the people enter.

Four PT members and Pastor: Lead the Call to Worship.
1. "Water of Life" (Townley) CC, 79
2. "Let Your Spirit Rise Within Me" (Speir) SFPW, 235
3. "Sing Unto the Lord" (unknown) SFPW, 23

WL: Give a spoken introduction to the prayer song.
4. "Only by Grace" (Gustafson) CCB, 42

Pastor: Lead congregational prayer time.

(10 min.) Special music with interpretive dance (choose a song of baptism or the the Holy Spirit). *(See music suggestions.)*

WL: Read the scripture (Matt. 3:13-17) from *THE MESSAGE* (Eugene Peterson).
5. "Baptized in Water" (Traditional/Saward) TCH, 465
6. "Spirit Song" (Wimber) CCB, 51

(25 min.) **Pastor:** Facilitate the sermon time. Four people from the congregation will share their baptism stories. *(See sermon notes.)*

(10 min.) **Response to the Word/Reaffirmation of Baptism**
As the people come forward, show the text of Matthew 3:13-17 (no sound) while playing recorded music and/or show pictures of people being baptized.
Optional music: "Holy Ground," performed by Barbra Streisand.

Pastor or WL: Benediction

Music Sources: *Come Celebrate!* (Abingdon Press); *Songs for Praise & Worship* (Word); *Cokesbury Chorus Book* (Abingdon Press); *The Celebration Hymnal* (Word/Integrity)

CALL TO WORSHIP

PT#1: We have come to this place expecting heaven to open for us.

PT#2: Heaven has already opened for us.

PT#3: We want to hear God speak.

PT#4: God has already spoken.

Pastor: When Jesus was baptized, God opened the heavens and a voice said, "This is my Son, chosen and marked by my love, delight of my life."

People: We, too, are chosen and marked by God's love. We are the delight of God's life.

BENEDICTION

L: You are chosen and marked by God's love.

P: I am chosen and marked by God's love.

L: You are the delight of God's life.

P: I am the delight of God's life.

L: Go into the world and live as chosen and marked people.

All: Hallelujah, Amen!

ALTAR

A white cloth covers the altar. In the center is a running water fountain. On the left is a blue bowl filled with water and floating candles. On the right is a seashell-shaped bowl filled with seashells, which the people will receive. Ten yards of aqua tulle is draped around the altar and on the floor. Silk ferns are used as the backdrop.

OPTIONS

Music

"Come, Be Baptized" (Smith) *Cokesbury Chorus Book* (Abingdon Press)

"Create in Me a Clean Heart" (Anon.) *Cokesbury Chorus Book* (Abingdon Press)

"Spirit of the Living God" (Iverson) *Cokesbury Chorus Book* (Abingdon Press)

"Waterlife" (Hanson) *Come Celebrate!* (Abingdon Press)

Recordings

"He Is All You Need" as performed by Steve Camp, from *Doin' My Best, Vol. 1* (Sparrow Records)

"Love That Will Not Let Me Go" as performed by Steve Camp, from *Doin' My Best, Vol. 1* (Sparrow Records)

SERMON

Idea Generator

In most congregations there is a diversity of church backgrounds. Each person has a unique and individual faith story. As preparation for this service, which focuses on baptism, it might be helpful for the pastor to write his or her own baptismal story. Because the service's intent is to remember your baptism, it might also be time for the pastor to review the church's theological understanding of baptism. The pastor might consider how to use the language of the culture to develop a balanced understanding and appreciation for the sacrament of baptism. A good resource is found in *The United Methodist Book of Worship* (pp. 81-85).

Introduction

(Because this service uses the individual baptismal stories to highlight the larger Christian story, a good introduction might include a highlight of the literal and symbolic role of water in scripture. You might choose to write this on your own. Consider using this adaptation from The United Methodist Book of Worship *and begin the sermon as follows.)*

"When nothing existed but chaos, God swept across the dark waters and brought forth light. In the days of Noah, God saved those on the ark through water. After the flood God set in the clouds a rainbow. When God saw the Hebrew people as slaves in Egypt, God led them to freedom through the sea. Their children God brought through the Jordan to the land which had been promised. In the fullness of time God sent Jesus, nurtured in the water of a womb. Jesus was baptized by John and anointed by God's Spirit." (Adapted from *The United Methodist Book of Worship*, p. 90.)

Body

(Four people were prepared to tell their baptism stories: an adult baptized as an infant; an adult baptized as an adult; an adult recalling his or her own children's baptisms; an adult baptized as a teenager. The pastor can tie these stories together and cue the next story with the words: "Remember your baptism and be thankful." The pastor's role in this service is to theologically connect all four baptism stories. The following ideas are how the themes might be developed.)

Our baptism stories are unique because we are unique, and yet we find a common story that connects us all as a community of faith. The images of baptism are the images from everyday life. Birth, putting on new clothes, getting clean, death, and burial are ordinary occurrences that happen in the course of a given life. However, these images become powerful symbols for what happens to us through our baptism.

The literal act of putting water on our head or being lowered into a pool of water does not mean we have performed a magic trick. Baptism is an outward sign of an inward and invisible grace. What we observe with our eyes is a symbolic action representing the action God has performed in our lives. Baptism is not something we do or the pastor does. Baptism is something God does. When we remember our baptism, we are not only looking at a historical event in our lives, we are also remembering God's faithfulness. We remember what God has done, what God is doing, and what God will do.

Conclusion

Not everyone has had the opportunity to tell their baptism story to the congregation, but everyone here will have the opportunity to reflect upon and remember their baptism. Remember your baptism and be thankful.

Prayer over Water

Pour out your Holy Spirit,
And by this gift of water call to our remembrance
The grace declared to us in our baptism.
(*The United Methodist Book of Worship,* p. 113)

RESPONSE TO THE WORD

You are invited, as you feel comfortable, to come forward and remember your baptism. You may touch the water and, if desired, touch your forehead. You may also pick up a shell to take home so that you can remember your baptism daily. If anyone present would like to receive the sacrament of baptism, you may speak to one of the pastors at either side of the stage. Come and remember your baptism and be thankful.

NOTES

Overcoming Your Fears

Ordinary Time

(15 min.)   **Call to Worship Movie Clip:** *What About Bob?* (Touchstone Pictures)

Description: The first meeting of Bob and Dr. Marvin in the doctor's office
Start Time: 8:15
Start Cue: Bob says, "Why don't I start?"
End Time: 9:34
End Cue: Dr. Marvin says, "What is it you are truly afraid of?"

Call to Worship Skit: *What Is Your Fear?*

(20 min.)   **Pastor:** Sermon

(15 min.)   **Solo:** "Greater Are You" (Altrogge) People of Destiny International, 1997

Pastor: Lead pastoral prayer time.

WL: Lead Litany.
    1. "He Is Jehovah" (Robinson) SFPW, 227
    2. "The Lord Is My Light" (Harrah) PHC, 156

Faith witness is given by a congregational member. Focus on "When God has helped me through a fearful time."

(5 min.)   **WL:** Ask the ushers forward to receive the offering.
    3. "You Are My Hiding Place" (Ledner) SFPW, 230
    4. "Jehovah to Me" (Keesecker) SFPW, 231

Time of Commitment
    5. "The Lord Is My Light" (Nelson) SFPW, 209

Pastor or WL: Benediction

Music Sources: *Songs for Praise and Worship* (Word); *Praise Hymns & Choruses* (Maranatha)

CALL TO WORSHIP SKIT: *What Is Your Fear?*
(Pastor and four PT members)

*(Talk show music begins as the **Pastor** enters and says, "Today we are going to talk about overcoming your fears." Music continues as the **PT** members enter and are seated in the chairs on the platform next to the talk show host [**Pastor**]. Music fades as everyone is seated.)*

Host: Ask each person what their biggest fear is and then respond briefly to each. Your response should state that this is what we will be looking at in depth during the show.

Fears could be the following or include your own:
1. Losing my job, not able to provide for my family
2. My children choosing the wrong path such as drugs, unprotected sex, and so on.
3. I, or someone in my family, getting cancer or other incurable disease.
4. Loss of personal safety; random acts of violence

*(At the conclusion of the interviews, the **PT** members should move off the platform as the sermon begins.)*

LITANY

L: When fear darkens the path of my life and I can't see where I'm going, I will remember:
P: The Lord is my Light.
L: When I wander aimlessly, lost and confused, I will remember:
P: The Lord is my Salvation.
L: When enemies seek to overwhelm and take control, I will remember:
P: The Lord is my Stronghold.
All: In God's house there is no confusion, no doubt, no fear. God is my salvation.

BENEDICTION

Remember, the Lord is your Light, your salvation, and your stronghold. You have nothing to fear. Hallelujah, Amen!

ALTAR

There is no altar for this service. The platform was set to look like a talk show, using chairs and plants.

OPTIONS

Music

"Ah, Lord God" (Chance) *Songs for Praise & Worship* (Word)
"His Strength Is Perfect" (Chapman/Salley) *The Celebration Hymnal* (Word/Integrity)
"Lord, I'm in Your Hands" (Weeks) *Praise Hymns & Choruses, 4th ed.* (Maranatha)
"My Life Is in You, Lord" (Gardner) *Songs for Praise & Worship* (Word)
"The Battle Belongs to the Lord" (Owens, Collins) *Songs for Praise & Worship* (Word)
"You Are My All in All" (Jernigan) *Songs for Praise & Worship* (Word)

SERMON

Idea Generator

Think about the amount of change you have experienced in your lifetime. In my own life, which spans forty years, I am amazed at all the changes. A startling example of this change is right in front of me. While in college in the 1970s, the computer lab contained a giant computer, which filled a space twenty feet square. Today, I am typing these words on a small personal computer with a memory capacity that far exceeds the computer of my college years.

In your congregation, there are people my age and older who have been swept into this millennium at a terrifying pace. The amount of change they have experienced is overwhelming. Change elicits fear and anxiety. What can we rely on in this dizzying culture of change? Are there eternal truths that are unchangeable? As pastoral preparation for the sermon, visit someone who is eighty to ninety years old. Ask that person to talk about the changes he or she has experienced over his or her lifetime.

Next, visit with someone twenty or under and ask the same questions. Those who are twenty and under are very adaptable to the change in technology and society structure. Or are they? The longing for stability and safety is apparent to anyone who spends time in conversation with this age group. Perhaps the needs and fears of the two age groups (over eighty and under twenty) are closer than we think.

Scripture is timeless. Even though we share the message in new and different ways, the message holds meaning and truth for every generation. God's ultimate truth can be shared in many formats, but truth is always truth.

Introduction

> The only thing we have to fear is fear itself—nameless, unreasoning, unjustified terror which paralyzes needed efforts to convert retreat into advance. (Franklin Delano Roosevelt, First Inaugural Address, March 4, 1933)

"The only thing we have to fear is fear itself." We have heard that quote from our collective memory many times and yet how many of us have heard the rest of the quote, "nameless, unreasoning, unjustified terror which paralyzes needed efforts to convert retreat into advance." If we wanted to give a definition of fear, I don't think we could define fear any better. Fear is nameless. It is hard to put a finger or a face on fear. Fear is unreasoning. Fear causes us to experience unjustified terror because it clouds any hope in the future. Fear paralyzes. When we need to move ahead, fear causes us to sound the call of retreat.

But God does not intend for people to live in a state of fear. "For God has not given us a spirit of fear, but of power and of love and of a sound mind" (2 Tim. 1:7 NKJV).

Body

The writer of Psalm 27 knew something about fear. The questions that are found in the psalm are those of a person who has struggled with fear. "Whom shall I fear? Of whom shall I be afraid?" However, the writer also knew without a doubt the source of hope and strength. The future was not fearful because the writer trusted in God. The psalmist identifies three aspects of God's faithfulness: Light, Salvation, and Stronghold.

The Lord is our light. Do you know what fear does? It makes everything dark and unclear. In Hebrew, the words light and fear are very similar. The similarities remind us how easy it is to slip into fear or darkness from light.

Think about driving on a dark lonely road. Your headlights go out. You become afraid and begin to panic. But the road is still there, you just can't see it without light. The road is always

present, but our fears cause the light of our souls to go dim. The psalmist reminds us of our light source. It is the Lord. We are not alone and our faith in the Almighty is our strength.

The words from Mark 5:36, "Do not fear, only believe" suggest, as does the psalmist, that the opposite of faith is fear. We tend to think of the opposite of faith as unbelief, but perhaps unbelief is really fear in disguise. We do not believe in the present. We do not believe in the future. We do not believe that there is a God who cares and has the best for us. That can cause fear.

The Lord is our salvation. The psalmist also reminds us that our salvation is found in the Lord. Perhaps we have our own baggage associated with the word salvation, but in biblical terms, salvation means life, especially life made possible when death is threatening.

The Lord is our stronghold. God is our protection. Does that mean we will be free from bad things happening in our life? No, our life is unfortunately subjected to the decisions we make and the decisions of those in our society. A man takes a gun and starts shooting children in a day care center. We don't have a God-shield to protect us from these kinds of things. But we don't have to be fearful for each day, because God is the ultimate victor. Nothing can separate us from the love of God, not even death.

Conclusion

For many of us, the changes in our society, the changes in our family, and even the changes in our church represent an uncertainty about the future. The psalmist's words are as important and essential to our time as to that ancient time in which they were written. God does not change. "The Lord is my light and my salvation; whom shall I fear? The Lord is the stronghold of my life; of whom shall I be afraid?" (Ps. 27:1).

NOTES _____

_____

_____

_____

_____

The Mirror of Love

Communion

(10 min.)   **Call to Worship Skit:** *What Is Love?*
1. "We Celebrate" (Till & Davenport) SFPW, 162
2. "Behold What Manner of Love" (Van Tine) SFPW, 48
3. "The Steadfast Love of the Lord" (McNeill) SFPW, 185
4. "Antiphonal Praise" (Green) SFPW, 25

WL: Lead unison Prayer of Confession.
5. "With All My Heart" (Mason) SFPW, 187

(10 min.)   **Pastor:** Lead congregational prayer time.

Faith witness is given by a congregational member. Focus on "What God's love looks like in my life."

(10 min.)   Scripture lesson is presented (1 Cor. 13). As the scripture is read by someone who cannot be seen by the congregation, another person removes the items from the altar that correspond to the scripture (cymbals, knowledge, mountain, wealth). *(See altar instructions.)*

PT Skit: *What Love Is Not*
6. "I Love You, Lord" (Klein) SFPW, 72

Pastor: Prepare the altar for communion during the song at the conclusion of the skit. The communion elements could be brought forward by members of the congregation.

(15 min.)   **Pastor:** Sermon

(15 min.)   **Pastor:** Consecrate the communion elements. While communion is being served, use the song "Gift of Love" as an anthem, PT special, or solo. (Hopson, UMH, 408)

Offerings may be brought forward during this time.

PT: Begin closing song from the back as a solo and add voices gradually.
7. "They'll Know We Are Christians" (vv. 1, 3, 4) CCB, 78

Pastor: Benediction

Music Sources: *Songs for Praise & Worship* (Word); *Cokesbury Chorus Book* (Abingdon Press); *The United Methodist Hymnal* (UMPH)

CALL TO WORSHIP SKIT: *What Is Love?*

(A couple enters the pastor's office for premarital counseling.)

Pastor: [Names], why do you want to get married?

Woman: Because I love him.

Man: *(Looking at the woman)* I love you!

(The couple continues with the back and forth "I love you" until the pastor interrupts.)

Pastor: [Woman's Name], what does love look like to you?

Woman: *(As if daydreaming)* A handsome fiancé with a fabulous job, a magnificent wedding, a home in an exclusive neighborhood, perfect children, and living happily ever after.

Pastor: *(To the man)* And what does love look like to you, [Man's Name]?

Man: *(Looking at the woman)* A beautiful woman with deep [state color] eyes, long flowing hair [or whatever hair type is appropriate], intelligent, always cheerful, dresses fashionably—our life is going to be perfect together!

Pastor: STOP!

(The couple freezes. The pastor looks at the couple in disbelief and then turns to the congregation.)

Pastor: What is your image of love?

PRAYER OF CONFESSION

Holy God, we rejoice that you have shown us the perfect image of love. Through Jesus' death and resurrection, we are recreated in your perfect image of love.

We confess, O God, our images of love are based on outward appearances, possessions, status symbols, and idealistic dreams. Our image of love is distorted by the bias of a superficial society. The truth is "Love is patient; love is kind; love is not envious or boastful or arrogant or rude. It does not insist on its own way; it is not irritable or resentful; it does not rejoice in wrongdoing, but rejoices in the truth. It bears all things, believes all things, hopes all things, endures all things" (1 Cor. 13:4-7).

Forgive us when we live a life of superficial love. Help us to reflect your image of perfect love. Amen.

PRAISE TEAM SKIT: *What Love Is Not*

Characters: Worship Leader in charge; six Praise Team members; Pastor to strike the gong; a scripture reader who is not seen by the congregation

(PT begins to lead the congregational song "I Love You, Lord" as usual, except the singers should sing in the key of F while the instruments play [very poorly] in the key of G. Continue this for approximately four to eight measures and then interrupt with the dialogue.)

WL: Stop, stop! This is terrible! What is wrong with you people?

PT#1: It might not have been our best effort, but if you hadn't stopped us, I'm sure we would have improved. I don't understand why we always have to go over and over it until we are sick and tired of singing. Sometimes you really ruin the song for all of us!

*(**Pastor** strikes gong.)* "Love is patient, love is kind."

PT#2: If I had been singing lead this would not have happened. I've tried to tell you a number of times that the strongest singer should always be the leader. But no, you insist on everyone having the opportunity. So see what happens?

*(**Pastor** strikes gong.)* "Love is not jealous or boastful."

PT#3: I thought I was doing just fine, thank you. It's the drummer that was getting us off. It's always the drummer. What is it with the drummer attitude? Drummers want you to think that they are the only ones who can really lead the song. I think someone needs to bring them down a notch or two!

(**Pastor** *strikes gong.*) "Love is not arrogant or rude."

PT#4: I just can't play this song in this terrible key. I keep telling you I can't play in this key so don't blame this problem on me. You would think that by now you could have changed it to a decent key for guitarists. If you are not going to pay any attention to me, I'll just take my guitar and go home.

(**Pastor** *strikes gong.*) "Love does not insist on it's own way."

PT#5: You are such a perfectionist. We can't ever please you. There is always something that you think needs to be fixed or could be better. I'm surprised you let us get up here to lead worship. You don't think we are ever good enough!

(**Pastor** *strikes gong.*) "Love is not irritable or resentful."

PT#6: I could have told you from the beginning that this wasn't going to work out. I knew it, anytime you put this many musicians together there will never be total agreement on how to do things. You would think everyone knows that!

(**Pastor** *strikes gong.*) "Love does not rejoice in wrong. *(Pause)* Love always protects, always trusts, always hopes, always perseveres. Love never fails."

(Begin the song "I Love You, Lord" [this time correctly]. Sing two times while the altar is prepared for communion.)

PRAYER OF CONSECRATION

Jesus said the greatest commandment is this: "You shall love the Lord your God with all your heart, and with all your soul, and with all your mind, and with all your strength. . . . You shall love your neighbor as yourself" (Mark 12:30-31). As a reminder of God's great love for us, this bread is a symbol of Jesus' body, which was broken for us, and this cup is a symbol of Jesus' blood, which was poured out for us. When we do this in remembrance of him we are recipients of God's great love. By your Holy Spirit,

bless this bread and wine. Through this reminder of your love, help us mirror your love to the world. Amen.

BENEDICTION

Will they know you are a Christian by your love? Do you mirror love? Remember, to love and to be loved is the greatest joy on earth. Hallelujah, Amen!

ALTAR

The altar is covered with a white cloth. The white banner in the middle, with a red heart and a black cross, can be easily made without sewing. A thirty-six-inch mirror is placed in the middle with three pillar candles (faith, hope, and love) in front of it. Four items on the altar that correspond to the scripture will be removed as the scripture is read *(see the script)*. These are: (1) cymbal; (2) stack of books; (3) mountain; and (4) treasure box. Also, the faith, hope, love candles are lighted at the end of the scripture reading. A gong is placed on the floor in front of the altar for use during the skit, *What Love Is Not. (If you do not have a gong, use a gong sound on an electronic keyboard.)* After these four items are removed, the communion elements are placed on the altar. As the people come forward for communion, they should be able to see themselves in the mirror.

OPTIONS

Music ♫

"Amazing Love" (Kendrick) *Come & Worship* (Integrity)

"Christ in Us Be Glorified" (Chapman) *Praise Hymns & Choruses (4th ed.)* (Maranatha)

"I Love You with the Love of the Lord" (Gilbert) *Songs for Praise & Worship* (Word)

"Let It Be Said of Us" (Fry) *Praise Hymns & Choruses (4th ed.)* (Maranatha)

"Make Us One" (Cymbala) *Praise Hymns & Choruses (4th ed.)* (Maranatha)

"More Love, More Power" (Hierrs) *Praise Hymns & Choruses (4th ed.)* (Maranatha)

"My Jesus, I Love Thee" (Featherstone/Gordon) *Praise Hymns & Choruses (4th ed.)* (Maranatha)

Recordings

"What Love Is" as performed by Out of the Grey on *Diamond Days* (Sparrow)

"Amazing Love/Greater Love" as performed on Praise Band 5 *Tell the World* (Maranatha)

"Your Everlasting Love" as performed on Praise Band 4 *Let The Walls Fall Down* (Maranatha)

Drama

Love Is a Cliché by Dave McClellan, Cross Point Script #11240. *(See introduction for resource.)* (Man and woman, five to six minutes)

Purpose: This sketch is used best to bring up the subject of romantic love and show how the music industry gives us distorted messages of what love actually is. Composed entirely from the lines of popular songs, it is unapologetically comic.

SERMON

Idea Generator

A pastor friend of mine uses 1 Corinthians 13 as a checklist for his own spiritual inventory. First he thinks of a person he professes to love; for example, his daughter. Is he patient and kind toward her? Does he bear all things, believe all things, hope all things, endure all things? It may appear easy at first glance. Of course we exhibit the characteristics of love with those who are closest to us. Or do we? Many times the ones who are closest to us receive the most unloving treatment from us.

The spiritual inventory does not stop here. Next, my friend thinks of a person with whom he may be in conflict. Again, do his actions, words, and even his thoughts exhibit the love described in 1 Corinthians 13? Is he patient and kind? Does he bear all things, believe all things, hope all things, endure all things? Does he keep track of who is right and who is wrong?

Try this checklist yourself and grade yourself by the standard of love found in 1 Corinthians 13.

Introduction

Several years ago, the city where I live came to a virtual standstill due to an unexpected severe snowstorm. Most in the city were without power for nearly a week. During that week, I found myself reluctant to even look in the mirror. Unwashed, dirty clothes, no makeup and tired, I looked awful. Some of my friends didn't recognize me at first glance.

The text helps us to be keenly aware of the characteristics of love and how we as Christians reflect or look like love. Do people recognize us as loving Christians? Do we as a community of faith reflect a spirituality that is based on the love described in 1 Corinthians 13? Would people look at our church and know what love looks like?

Too often the community of faith becomes a place where decisions are made based on the power of persuasion, strength of the pocketbook, or the voice that is the loudest, rather than matters of the heart. We may proclaim the importance of sharing our resources with the poor, but does that extend to opening our beautiful church buildings for "those people" to find shelter?

During that snowstorm, the church in which I pastor opened its doors to anyone who needed shelter. For many of us who take the basic necessities of life for granted, it was an eye-opening experience. I understood concretely the kind of love that is described in 1 Corinthians 13. It is sacrificial and does not count the cost.

Body

The service began by looking at what love is *not* rather than trying to describe what love *is*. Many voices try to define for us this elusive quality of love (television, movies, pop songs), thus turning the concept of love into a syrupy ideal or a distorted self-centered action based on our own wants and desires.

When most people think of love, they think of the love between a man and a woman. Millions and millions of people pledge their love to each other for all eternity as they marry. Statistics tell us that one-half of those commitments will end in divorce.

Perhaps it is easy to understand what love is by recognizing what love is not, because many of us have experienced what love is not more often than the type of love described by Paul in the New Testament. Everyday, people come to my office asking me to help them with their problems when all they really want is to be loved. That seems like such a simplistic idea, but it's important that we understand that people want to be loved in the manner of 1 Corinthians 13.

In a society that associates physical beauty with the worthiness to be loved, most people buy into their unworthiness based on this superficial value. Little girls learn to starve themselves and develop eating disorders because magazines project an image that to be loved one must be abnormally thin. The love ethic of 1 Corinthians 13 reminds us that love can be seen, but it has nothing to do with physical appearance.

So what does love look like? In the movie *Dead Man Walking,* based on the life of Sister Helen Prejean, Sister Helen is a reflection of the love founded on her Christian value system. She tells convicted killer Matthew Poncelet before he is to be executed, "I want the last face you see in this world to be the face of love, so you look at me when they do this thing. I'll be the face of love for you." Sister Helen is what love looks like.

What does love look like? It looks like a couple who have just celebrated their sixtieth wedding anniversary. They are no longer the young idealistic couple who gazed at each other with starry-eyed wonder. They have survived and grown through tragedy and hardship. They have decided to believe in for better or for worse. Despite health problems, gray hair, and hearing loss, they still would choose each other to make a life and home.

What does love look like? Love is a parent welcoming a child who has told the parent that he or she is homosexual. Nothing can change the parent's love for this child.

What does love look like? Love is a community of faith where someone's past is not important or remembered and someone's future is embraced with hope and promise.

What does love look like? Love is Jesus the Christ who would choose to die so that you and I might have life.

What does love look like? Love looks like you.

NOTES

A New Life in a New Land

Ordinary Time

(10 min.)   **Pastor:** Introduction to the service.

Call to Worship Skit: *Packing for a Move*

(10 min.)   **PT:** Lead songs and read scripture between songs. *(Read from THE MESSAGE by Eugene Peterson, if possible.)*
     1. "Let Your Spirit Rise Within Me" (Speir) SFPW, 235

WL#1: Scripture reading #1 (Rom. 6:1-4)
     2. "Lord, I Lift Your Name on High" (Founds) CCB, 36
     3. "In Him We Live" (Speir) SFPW, 205

WL#2: Scripture reading #2 (Rom. 6:11)
     4. "I Am Not My Own" (Nystrom) SB#6, 491
     5. "Hallowed Be Thy Name" (Mason/Lawson) SFPW, 41

WL#1: Scripture reading #3 (Rom. 6:12-14)
     6. "When I Look into Your Holiness" (Perrin) SFPW, 71

(10 min.)   **Pastor:** Lead congregational prayer time.

Faith Witness: Ask a member of the congregation to share how he or she is living in the freedom of God.

(20 min.)   **Pastor:** Sermon

(10 min.)   **Special Music:** Have a solo, **PT** special, or anthem while the offering is being received. Choose a song that focuses on living the new life in the Lord. *(See Music Options.)*

PT: Lead closing song.
     7. "For This Purpose" (Kendrick) SFPW, 125

Pastor: Benediction

Music Sources: *Songs for Praise & Worship* (Word); *Cokesbury Chorus Book* (Abingdon Press); *Praise Songbook #6* (Integrity)

INTRODUCTION TO THE SERVICE

If you are like most people, the only time you seriously discard old, useless items is when you are preparing to move from one place to another. We want to start fresh and clean in our new home or place of business. So how do you inventory and decide what to take with you? Maybe this is more of a spiritual decision than you think.

CALL TO WORSHIP SKIT: *Packing for a Move*

Characters: A husband and wife; Pastor

Props: A moving box and a pile of "stuff" to be packed. (Include: a worn-out shirt with holes; a movie ticket stub; a broken flashlight; a stack of papers.)

(The couple is folding clothes and packing them in the box while also discarding a few into the "discard" pile.)

Woman: *(Holding up the worn-out shirt)* I don't think so! *(She starts to throw it in discard pile.)*

Man: Hey, wait a minute! You can't throw that away!

Woman: Why not? It's old, holey, and smelly!

Man: But this represents some of the best times of my life! See this hole? That happened at the annual fraternity football game. And this tear? Well, after the game, remember that really cool party? That was *some* party!

Woman: *(Exasperated)* No, I *don't* remember that!

Man: *(Embarrassed)* Oops, well . . . *(He holds up the movie ticket stubs.)* What about these? *(Motions to the discard pile.)*

Woman: Wait a minute! Don't throw those away! *(Reminisces.)* That was one of the best nights of my life. It was the first time . . . *(Looks at her husband.)* Oh, sorry. *(Both continue placing "stuff" in the box.)* Now this! *(Holds up a broken flashlight.)* You have kept this broken flashlight far too long!

Man: I know, but I still might fix it. *(Continues to mumble about how good the flashlight was.)*

Woman: *(Sarcastically)* You always do have good intentions.

Man: *(Holds up notebook papers.)* Now why, in heaven's name, would you save these old college papers?

Woman: *(Self-righteously)* They remind me of how smart I really am. I made the highest grade in my class. I was always the best; in fact, my professor always said to me . . .

Man: *(Interrupting)* Yeah, yeah, yeah! I've heard it all before! *(Dumps everything else in the box and freezes.)*

Pastor: I believe these two need to think about what they should leave behind. After all, they are moving to a new place and making a new start. It's like a new life in a new land.

BENEDICTION

I see it! *(Pointing in the distance)*. I see a new life in a new land. I see a new country of grace. So let's move in. Hallelujah, Amen.

ALTAR

Make a simple banner with a butterfly (a symbol for new life) cut out of felt and glued to a felt background (no sewing necessary). Matching color felt hangs from the center music stand. A large pot of yellow chrysanthemums is placed in the center with two pillar candles inside hurricane lamps on either side. Silk ferns and ivy are used as filler.

OPTIONS

Music ♫
"Change My Heart, O God" (Espinosa) *Cokesbury Chorus Book* (Abingdon Press)
"Create in Me a Clean Heart" (Anon.) *Cokesbury Chorus Book* (Abingdon Press)
"Hide Me in Your Holiness" (Ragsdale) *Praise Hymns & Choruses (4th ed.)* (Maranatha)
"I Need You" (Founds) *Praise Hymns & Choruses (4th ed.)* (Maranatha)

Recordings

"I Can Begin Again" as performed by Larnelle Harris, from *The Very Best: Top 10 Gospel Songs* (Sony/Word)

"Winds of Change" as performed by Russ Taff, from *The Way Home* (Myrrh Records)

SERMON

Idea Generator

In Eugene Peterson's *THE MESSAGE*, the new life in Christ is described as moving to a new country. There are some wonderful resources on the Internet (use the search word *immigrants*) that give a vivid picture of what it is like to move from one country to another. One of the important elements of our faith is the radical movement from sin to grace. What does this new land of grace look like? How can we describe this new way of life to our congregation? The concept of leaving the old country behind and moving to a new land is the continuing story of God's relationship with God's people. We find this theme throughout the scriptures. As a spiritual exercise, the pastor might take time this week to look at the stories from scripture that give flesh to this theme.

(This is a good opportunity to use an outline with the congregation. The following is an outline that can be used. Comments are provided that will give a general direction of the particular points. The bold-faced portions can be printed and handed out to the congregation as a handout to take home. Also, the outline may be displayed on a video-projection screen.)

I. Leaving the old country (Rom. 6:1-2)

There are a variety of reasons why one chooses to move to a new country. For the Christian, it is a realization that when one resides in sin it is like living under the constraints of a tyranny. A good example are those who fled Germany during the rise of Hitler and Nazism.

  A. It doesn't fit anymore (Eph. 4:22-23)
  One decides to move to another place because the current residence doesn't seem to fit the direction of one's life. A good comparison is looking at the clothes in our closets. Old clothes in the closet might be too snug or out of style. You don't feel good

in them. The Christian will find the old lifestyle uncomfortable. It just doesn't fit.

  B. The right fit (Luke 24:29; 2 Cor. 5:4)
  The journey begins to find the place where life seems free and natural. It must be the right fit. If the old lifestyle doesn't fit, then we must find what does seem natural and comfortable. This is Holy Spirit clothing.

II. The Journey (Rom. 6:7-14)

How does one begin the journey? Paul looks at the mode of transportation as baptism. Baptism, the outward sign of an inward grace, is the mode of transport to the land of grace. Our baptismal calling gives us the direction. *(This is an appropriate time to remind the congregation of the vows made at baptism.)*

  A. The mode of transportation (Col. 2:12)
  The mode of transportation is unusual in that it means we spiritually die to the old ways and rise to a new way. How we used to travel isn't sufficient anymore. How many of us have discovered a better way of going to a well-traveled location? You don't want to go back and travel the old way because a better way has been found.

  B. We must die to live (1 Pet. 3:21; 2 Cor. 4:8-12)
  This is one of the paradoxes of scripture. To gain life we must lose our life. We must die to live. We have to die to our own desires, ambitions, and boundaries. In dying we are changed to enable us to live as children of the kingdom.

III. The New Land (Rom. 6:7-14)

Now that we know how we can travel to the new land, what will the new land look like? When an immigrant arrives in this country, there are conditions and regulations with which the person must adhere. The immigration office gives the new resident many papers of information. The new land of grace has only one principle: Jesus' death on the cross provides all the information that one needs to begin life in the new land.

  A. Geography (Rom. 14:17)
  Geography is the study of the features of an area. The features of this new land are the characteristics of God. We are no longer focused on the temporal pleasures of our

current lifestyle. Our lives become grounded in the eternal characteristics of righteousness, peace, and joy.

B. Language (1 Cor. 13:1)

We have to learn a new language in this new country. The new language is love. Our old language helped us communicate a value system that was narcissistic and self-destructive. Now we communicate differently. Just as words from one language to another have different meanings and nuances, words of the kingdom take on the nuance of love.

C. Customs (Gal. 5:22-23)

As I was preparing to go on a mission trip to another country, I was instructed by our leader about certain customs of which we should be aware. These were guidelines to help us be more effective in our relationship with the people we would be meeting. We would not want to do anything inappropriate that would cause distress to our hosts. The customs of the new land to which we are moving are defined as fruit. They are guidelines on how we are to be in relationship with one another.

IV. Conclusion

Why do we move to this new land? We move for freedom. We move for opportunity and for growth. We move for life.

NOTES _____

Who Is This?

(10 min.)	**Call to Worship Skit:** *Why Did You Come?*

Pastor: Lead Call to Worship.

PT: Lead the opening songs.
1. "His Name Is Life" (Licciardello/Gaither) SFPW, 88
2. "King of Kings" (Conty/Batya) SFPW, 94
3. "Glory to the King" (McLain) SFPW, 83

(10 min.) **Pastor or WL:** Read Invocation.
4. "Blessed Be the Name of the Lord" (Moen) SFPW, 80
5. "Worthy, You Are Worthy" (Moen) SFPW, 81

Pastor: Lead congregational prayer time.
6. "O Lord, You're Beautiful" (Green) SFPW, 178

(20 min.) Run video *(The Visual Bible)* or read Matthew 21:1-11.

Pastor: Sermon

(10 min.) **PT:** Lead songs while waving palms.
7. "Hosanna" (Tuttle) SFPW, 82
8. "Lift Up Your Heads" (Fry) SFPW, 127

Pastor: Conclusion to sermon (Passion story)

(10 min.) **Response to the Word**

Solo: "Lamb of God" (Paris) SFPW, 112
(During the solo, the pastor should remove fabric from the cross [if the cross is used] and drop a palm branch at the foot of the cross. People from the congregation may also come forward to place their palm at the foot of the cross.)

PT: Lead the closing song.
9. "O How He Loves You and Me" (Kaiser) SFPW, 113

WL or Pastor: Benediction

Music Sources: *Songs for Praise & Worship* (Word)

CALL TO WORSHIP SKIT: *Why Did You Come?*

Characters: A television interviewer; Jesus (dressed in shabby clothes over a white robe); three couples: (1) Academy award winners; (2) Proud parents; (3) Snobbish couple.

(The first couple enters from the back and walks down the aisle arm in arm, as if they are entering the Academy Awards ceremony [they should be very well dressed]. The interviewer is standing at the end of the aisle with the microphone ready.)

Interviewer: What a beautiful couple. Look, I believe it's [names]. *(To the couple)* Where did you get those beautiful clothes?

Woman #1: I'm so glad that you noticed. I spent, I mean *we* spent many long hours shopping for just the right attire. *(Continues to talk about the clothes as they both move to the front.)*

(The second couple enters.)

Interviewer: Here's another couple entering. Excuse me, can I ask why you are coming to this Palm Sunday service?

Woman #2: We wanted to see our children parade with the palms. You know, their names will be in the bulletin. I think they are so cute to watch.

Interviewer: What do *you* expect to get out of the service today? *(They look confused, shrug their shoulders, and continue to talk about their precious children as they move to the front.)*

(The third couple enters.)

Interviewer: Here comes another. Excuse me, may I ask why you are coming to this Palm Sunday service? *(They ignore the interviewer and simply continue walking to the front.)* Well, maybe they are just in a hurry to find the perfect seats inside.

(Jesus enters. As he is walking in, the three couples are talking to themselves [loud enough to be heard], asking these questions: Who is he? Didn't anyone tell him about the dress code here? Someone needs to stop him

from coming in. Who does he think he is? The questions stop abruptly when Jesus turns to face the congregation [he has removed his shabby clothes to uncover a white robe] with his arms open wide.)

Interviewer: What would it be like if Jesus walked in here today like he rode into Jerusalem two thousand years ago?

CALL TO WORSHIP

L: Not glamour, glitz and gowns by Armani,
P: but the simplicity of a palm branch.
L: Not a Porsche with the latest plush options or even a sports utility vehicle,
P: but the very cheapest vehicle the nation knew.
L: Not raised in a palace with country club privileges,
P: but nurtured by a common carpenter and devout mother.
L: Who is this, who has never been on the Fortune 500 list, will never win an Oscar, Pulitzer Prize or a gold record?
P: Who is this?
L: Yes, who is this?
P: His name is Jesus.

INVOCATION

Jesus, our Lord and our God, why was your triumphal entry into Jerusalem on a donkey rather than a beautiful champion horse? Why did you enter with fisherman and children rather than kings, rabbis, and heads of states? Your type of humility is not what we expect from a king. Yet today we worship you as our Lord and King; we bow before you and spread our palm branches at your feet to honor you. May you truly be honored. Amen.

BENEDICTION

Our last image is the cross, but that is not the end of the story. Hallelujah, Amen.

ALTAR

White and purple fabrics are draped across the center of the altar onto the floor. An arrangement of three different types of palms is in the center. A large pillar candle on a gold candleholder is on either side. The large wooden cross to the left of the altar is draped with purple fabric. The congregation will drop their palm branches in front of this cross.

OPTIONS

Music 🎵
"Bless the Name of Jesus"(Licciardello) *Songs for Praise & Worship* (Word)

"His Name Is Life" (Licciardello/Gaither) *Songs for Praise & Worship* (Word)

"In the Name of the Lord" (Patti/McHugh/Gaither) *Songs for Praise & Worship* (Word)

"Praise to the Holy One" (Fry) *Songs for Praise & Worship* (Word)

"The Lion and the Lamb" (Barbour/Batstone) *Praise Hymns & Choruses (4th ed.)* (Maranatha)

"We Will Glorify" (Paris) *Cokesbury Chorus Book* (Abingdon Press)

"We Worship and Adore Thee" (Traditional) *Cokesbury Chorus Book* (Abingdon Press)

Recordings ▭
"Crown Him with Many Crowns" as performed by Michael W. Smith, from *I'll Lead You Home* (Reunion Records)

"How Could You Say No" as performed by Billy Sprague, from *I Wish* (Reunion Records)

SERMON

Idea Generator
What pastor has not stated in frustration: "Jesus couldn't even please the church today." This statement is the starting point for examining our hearts concerning our reaction to Jesus' presence in our lives, church, and community.

Contemporary worship services can sometimes fall into the trap of being inward spiritual, self-gratifying experiences. The music is upbeat. The sermons are focused on one's own personal spirituality. It is important that we be on guard so that we do not find ourselves moving away from the mandate of the gospel on a larger social scale by trying to always provide a feel-good, fuzzy experience.

This week the service starts with a question: How would we respond if Jesus literally walked into our service? It concludes with the answer: Society's rejection of Jesus' prophetic and demanding message. We begin with Hosannas and end with the Cross. Yet the Cross is not a symbol of defeat, but of God's faithfulness in spite of our faithlessness.

Introduction
What would it be like if Jesus did come to our service today? We asked that question at the beginning of the service. When Jesus entered into Jerusalem the crowds shouted "Hosanna!"

The word *Hosanna* was originally a prayer requesting God's help. The word was also associated with Jewish hopes for deliverance by a political hero. When shouted to Jesus by pilgrims and children, it indicates they saw in him the fulfillment of their messianic expectations. But Jesus came as a spiritual deliverer on a lowly donkey—not as a conquering military hero on a prancing horse. (*Nelson's Illustrated Bible Dictionary*, Nashville: Thomas Nelson Publishers, 1986)

Body
We would like to think we would sing and shout in praise if Jesus walked in the service today. But are our words a reflection of the condition of our heart? Jesus' message did not meet the expectations of those seeking a leader for the nation of Israel. We wonder if Jesus would meet the expectations that we are seeking for a church leader. Would our Staff Parish Relations Committee or Pastor Search Committee want a leader who expects us to invite poor people into our building? Would the committee want someone who consorted with people at the local bar? Would they want someone who sought and proclaimed healing for those who are HIV positive?

Perhaps it might not seem politically correct to say that we wouldn't want this type of leadership, but let's look at the standard response to what type of leadership is usually desired. If our church placed an advertisement in the paper for a pastoral leader, what qualities would they seek? A good fund-raiser, someone who can deliver a stirring message, a person who cares for the membership might be some of the qualities stated. But based on what we read about

Jesus and his ministry outside of organized religion to the outcasts and broken, would Jesus be a top choice for a pastoral leadership position in our church? The shouts of "Hosanna" begin to sound hollow in our ears when we examine these questions in our own personal context.

Conclusion (Passion)

At the beginning of the week, Jesus had arrived in Jerusalem in what is called the triumphal entry, but by the end of the week the mood had shifted dramatically. Everyone had deserted Jesus, even those closest to him. The palm branches that had been used as a symbol of victory have dried up and are only useful to be thrown into the fire.

Do we, like the crowds, know the right words to say and yet fail when it comes to the action of living out our faith? Do we wave our symbols of victory when it is convenient and the mood is favorable?

What would we do if Jesus were to walk into our church today? The question is not a rhetorical one because Jesus is here. Our palm branches lie at the foot of his cross as a reminder of how easy we speak about our faith and how faithful Jesus is as the source of our faith.

RESPONSE TO THE WORD

As a time of reflection, you are invited to bring your palm branch forward and place it at the foot of the cross. Remember God's faithfulness to you.

NOTES

While It Was Still Dark, the Son Had Already Risen

This service begins in darkness. The altar and cross are covered in black. There should be a quiet, somber mood set with very soft background music *(use rain forest sounds or cricket sounds)*. If you use video projection, have a picture of the three crosses displayed. Do not change the slide until the darkness has been removed and the service has moved into the light. If you have created a tomb *(see altar instructions)*, have the spotlight come on inside the tomb as the service moves to light.

(15 min.)   Interpretive dance to "Were You There?" (Traditional Spiritual) or "Son of Man" (Bird/Lacy) as performed by Eden's Bridge on *Celtic Praise*. *(The dance should conclude with the removing of all black fabric, lighting the Christ candle, and spotlighting the tomb. Then the Praise Team enters to lead the opening songs.)*
      1. "Christ the Lord Is Risen Today" (Wesley) UMH, 302
      2. "Lord, I Lift Your Name on High" (Founds) CCB, 36

    WL: Lead Call to Worship.
      3. "He Is Lord" (Traditional) SFPW, 122
      4. "Because He Lives" (Gaither) SFPW, 123
      5. "For This Purpose" (Kendrick) SFPW, 125

(15 min.)   **Pastor or WL:** Welcome the people and ask them to stand and greet one another as the resurrected people of Christ.

    WL: Lead the Affirmation of Faith.
      6. "Amazing Love" (Kendrick) TCH, 351

    Pastor: Lead the congregational prayer time.

    Solo: "Was It a Morning Like This?"
    (as performed by Sandi Patti on *Morning Like This*, Word)

(20 min.)   **Pastor:** Sermon

    Time of Reflection
    (PT Band plays one to two minutes of reflective music.)

(10 min.)   **Offering:** Choose an anthem, PT special, or solo appropriate for Easter *(see music and recording options)*.

    Pastor: Offer a time of commitment during the closing song.
      7. "For This Purpose" (Kendrick) SFPW, 125

    Pastor or WL: Lead Benediction.

Music Sources: *Songs for Praise & Worship* (Word); *The Celebration Hymnal* (Word/Integrity); *The United Methodist Hymnal* (UMPH); *Cokesbury Chorus Book* (Abingdon Press)

CALL TO WORSHIP

L: Can you see that the stone is rolled away?
P: Yes, He is risen!
L: Can you see that the tomb is empty?
P: Yes, He is risen!
L: Can you see that the tomb is filled with light?
P: Yes, He is risen!
L: He is risen indeed!
P: Hallelujah! He is risen indeed!

AFFIRMATION OF FAITH

We believe in an Easter God, who loves each of us so completely that an amazing sacrifice was given to transform us into a people of light.

We believe in the risen Christ, who showed us how to live as a people of light.

We believe in the Holy Spirit, who encourages us to live joyfully in the light.

We believe that we are God's Easter people, resurrected and renewed.

BENEDICTION

L: While it is still dark, the Son has already risen.
P: The Son has risen, indeed!
L: You are no longer people of darkness, for the risen Christ lives in you.
P: Hallelujah, the Light has come.
L: Go forth as Easter people to share the resurrection Light.
All: Hallelujah, Amen!

ALTAR

A white cloth covers the altar. Rocks of all sizes and shapes were collected from a riverbank and stacked on the altar. *(Be sure your table can handle the weight.)* A narrow piece of muslin is twisted and placed over the top of the rocks and down the sides. A crown of thorns is in the center of the rocks. Behind the rocks are six white candles in gold holders that are graduated in height. In the center is a white pillar candle. All of this will be draped with a very lightweight black fabric before the service begins. When the black fabric is removed, the center Christ candle will be lighted *(see script)*. To the left of the altar is a large eight-foot wooden cross with Easter lilies at the base.

A tomb is created by sponge painting a refrigerator box and cutting out the door. The door piece of cardboard is also painted and draped with muslin. Silk ivy is placed on top of the cardboard box to make it more realistic. The refrigerator box is attached to a black backdrop. A spotlight is placed inside the tomb for use during the service *(see script)*. Ferns and Easter lilies are placed on the floor in front of the tomb and altar.

OPTIONS

Music 🎵

"Alleluia! Alleluia!" (Wordsworth/Beethoven) *The Celebration Hymnal* (Word/Integrity)
"By His Grace" (Fry) *The Celebration Hymnal* (Word/Integrity)
"Celebrate Jesus" (Oliver) *The Celebration Hymnal* (Word/Integrity)
"He Is Exalted" (Paris) *Songs for Praise & Worship* (Word)
"I Live" (Cook) *Songs for Praise & Worship* (Word)

Recordings 📼

"Arise My Love" as performed by Newsong, from *People Get Ready* (Benson Records)
"Easter Song" as performed by Keith Green, from *The Ministry Years, Vol. 1* (Sparrow Records)
"Glorious Morning" as performed by Sandi Patti, from *Songs From the Heart* (Impact Records)
"He Has Risen" as performed by DeGarmo & Key, from *Communication* (Forefront Records)
"I've Just Seen Jesus" as performed by Larnelle Harris and Sandi Patti, from *Songs 4 Life: Renew Your Health!* (Madacy Records)
"Jesus Is Alive" as performed by Ron Kenoly, from *Jesus Is Alive* (Hosanna!/Integrity Records)
"The Victor" as performed by Steve Green, from *The Ministry Years, Vol. 1* (Sparrow Records)

SERMON

Idea Generator

Easter Sunday has arrived and the church is packed to overflowing capacity. Every preacher knows that this is the high point for any church. It's time to shout our praises: "He is risen!" But let's back up for just a second. What if we entered the church and the altar was bare and the lights were off. It is dark and quiet. After all, that is the way that morning began. Easter did not begin with a shout. Easter began with a sob.

Do we move too quickly into resurrection? Perhaps we do. Maybe we are so intent that the Good News be declared that we forget many of the members of the congregation have arrived in darkness. We have Good News to share, but like Jesus, the best place for the Good News to be received is at the point of our darkness.

Instructions: This sermon is presented as a first-person sermon, portraying the character of Mary Magdalene (in costume). In the following you will find the general idea of the first-person sermon, but research into Mary Magdalene may be helpful for the preacher to develop one's own style. The sermon can also work with a male (in biblical costume) recounting the story Mary told him. The idea of the sermon can also be incorporated into a more traditional sermon format.

Mary Magdalene

It was still dark as I hurried down the path of the cemetery. The darkness matched my heart and my spirit. There didn't seem to be any light left inside me. I wasn't aware of much around me other than my focus on my destination. My eyes were swollen and sore. I had cried so much and I didn't think I could possibly cry another tear. But everytime I let my mind wander over the events of the past week, the tears would come again.

I shivered in the cold morning air as I remembered. I remembered the first time I met Jesus. I remembered how he had healed me of the demons that tormented me. I remembered his words of love and goodness. I remembered his compassion and kindness.

And then I remembered Friday. What a terrible day that had been. I recalled Jesus entering into Jerusalem with shouts of praise and adoration. I remembered him being led up a hill and crucified on the cross. I had felt so helpless. What had happened?

I still felt helpless as I hurried to the tomb where Jesus had been buried. I couldn't do anything Friday, but maybe there would be something I could do for his burial.

Suddenly, I stopped short as I arrived at the place where I was told he had been buried. He had been placed in a tomb that had been sealed by a huge stone, but the stone had been removed. Something was wrong. I ran back to get Peter and the other disciple. They thought I was crazy and they ran to see for themselves. But they didn't try to explain anything, they just left.

I stayed and looked around dazed. Then I started crying again. This was getting worse. Jesus' body had disappeared. I looked inside the tomb and to my surprise I discovered I was not alone. The one who was inside was not Jesus, but he did inquire about my tears.

He didn't seem to understand my frustration. Where was the body? Outside the tomb I saw someone else and stopped him. He inquired about my tears also. I just needed to know where they had taken the body of Jesus.

Then he said it. He said my name: Mary. No one else could speak my name like Jesus, and my heart filled with joy. I cried, "Teacher," and tried to hold on to him. But Jesus was not the same, he could not be contained or held. He was different. Our relationship was going to be different. He was no longer my Teacher, he was now my Savior and Lord.

I realized all this later as I remembered that glorious day. Jesus instructed me to go tell his disciples and I ran back to tell them that I had seen the Lord. I was the first evangelist sharing the good news of Jesus' Resurrection.

I ran back up the path. The sun was brilliant. The flowers and trees were everywhere. The birds were singing with the joy of this new morning. Everything was bursting with life and suddenly I remembered something. Earlier I walked down this path and it was still dark. But, while it was still dark the Son had already risen.

I guess if you had to hear anything in this story, hear this. While it is still dark, the Son has already risen. When you experience rejection and it is hard to move on, remember, while it is still dark the Son has already risen (*light first candle*). When you are forced into early retirement and the future seems bleak, remember, while it is still dark the Son has already risen (*light second candle*). When the news the doctor gives you is bad, remember, while it is still dark the Son has already risen (*light third candle*). When a relationship has been wounded or severed, remember, while it is still dark the Son has already risen (*light fourth candle*). When your child makes bad life choices, remember, while it is still dark the

Son has already risen *(light fifth candle)*. When you are saying good-bye to someone who has died, remember, while it is still dark the Son has already risen *(light sixth candle)*.

I didn't know it that morning as I traveled down the path to the tomb. My heart was devastated, and the darkness matched my spirit. But whether I knew it or acknowledged it—the Son had already risen!

NOTES _____

_____

_____

_____

_____

Broken Pieces

A Service of Healing

(10 min.)   **Call to Worship Skit:** *A Broken Pot*

    1. "How Majestic Is Your Name" (Smith) SFPW, 14
    2. "Awesome Power" (Elliott) SFPW, 10
    3. "Awesome God" (Mullins) SFPW, 11

WL: Lead unison prayer.

    4. "I Exalt Thee" (Sanchez) SFPW, 18
    5. "Glorify Thy Name" (Adkins) SFPW, 19

(10 min.)   **Pastor:** Lead congregational prayer time.

Faith Witness: Ask a layperson to give a short witness about a
time God has healed his or her brokenness.

(25 min.)   **PT:** Lead songs of preparation.

    6. "He Is Jehovah" (Robinson) SFPW, 227
    7. "I Am the God that Healeth Thee" (Moen) SFPW, 232
    8. "Be Still and Know" (Anon.) SFPW, 49

Pastor: Sermon

(10 min.)   **Pastor:** Time of healing
The healing service in *The United Methodist Book of Worship* is a
good resource (pp. 613-22).
The people may come forward for a time of prayer and/or healing,
to pick up a broken piece and to give their tithes and offerings.
During this time a solo or recorded music should be used. *(See Music
Options.)*

PT: Lead the closing song.

    9. "Be Still and Know" (Anon.) SFPW, 49

WL or Pastor: Benediction

Music Sources: *Songs for Praise & Worship* (Word)

CALL TO WORSHIP SKIT: *A Broken Pot*

Characters: One person to carry the pot; Pastor; all Praise Team Singers

(A person carrying a medium to large size clay pot enters and walks to the front. This person appears to be overly excited and nervous about the placement of this pot. He or she drops the pot and it breaks. If you do not have a hard floor in your worship space that will guarantee the pot to be broken, prepare the pot with a few breaks ahead of time.)

*(The **PT** singers enter immediately and start picking up the broken pieces and putting them on the altar. At the same time, the pastor enters and says to the person, "That's all right, [name]. This sort of thing just happens. It's all a part of life. There is a lot of brokenness, but God can heal it all and sometimes God does it through our friends." The Pastor motions to **PT** singers.)*

*(As the **PT** members prepare to lead worship, the pastor says to the congregation, "Do you feel broken? As we worship, we offer our brokenness to God in whatever form that may be. God will gather us into the place of healing and restoration. Let us give thanks and praise to the God of healing.")*

PRAYER (UNISON)

Awesome God, we fumble through life and sometimes the things that are most important end up in broken pieces around us. We stand in the middle of our broken pieces remembering that you are the healer, the reconciler, and the mender of brokenness. Hear the cries of our hearts and allow our worship to bring us to wholeness in you. Amen.

BENEDICTION

Take your broken piece home and place it where you can see it daily as a reminder of Jesus' command to his disciples and to us, "pick up the broken pieces so that none will be lost." Amen.

ALTAR

Two Mexican-style blankets cover the altar. Four candles in metal holders are on the left side. A whole clay pot is in the center with three small votive candles in front of the pot. On the right side are two clay pots (large and small) laying on their sides with broken clay pot pieces inside. Multicolored stoles are used to decorate the center music stand and the two small tables in front of the altar. The broken pieces that will be picked up by members of the congregation are placed in the two baskets on the small tables in front of the altar.

OPTIONS

Music

"A Shield About Me" (Thomas/Williams) *Songs for Praise & Worship* (Word)

"Cares Chorus" (Willard) *Cokesbury Chorus Book* (Abingdon Press)

"Change My Heart, O God" (Espinosa) *Cokesbury Chorus Book* (Abingdon Press)

"Create in Me a Clean Heart" (Anon.) *Cokesbury Chorus Book* (Abingdon Press)

"People Need the Lord" (Nelson/McHugh) *Cokesbury Chorus Book* (Abingdon Press)

"Spirit Song" (Wimber) *Cokesbury Chorus Book* (Abingdon Press)

"You Are My All in All" (Jernigan) *Songs for Praise & Worship* (Word)

Recordings

"Bound to Come Some Trouble" as performed by Rich Mullins, from *Never Picture Perfect* (Reunion Records)

"Hiding Place" as performed by Steven Curtis Chapman, from *First Hand* (Sparrow Records)

"Remember Not" as performed by Susan Ashton, from *Susan Ashton* (Sparrow Records)

"Weak Days" as performed by Steven Curtis Chapman, from *First Hand* (Sparrow Records)

Healing Service

Blessed to Be a Blessing by James K. Wagner, published by The Upper Room

SERMON

Idea Generator

I often think, around noon on Sunday of the "feeding of the five thousand" story. People are starting to look at their watches. Children are getting more and more restless. Did you ever wonder what it must have been like for Jesus on that late afternoon by the Sea of Galilee? We know from experience that when people are hungry they start to get agitated. I always look out on those Sunday mornings and think of how we can be used to bring healing and wholeness. I think Jesus' instructions to his disciples have significance to all of us who try to live out our calling as pastor-preachers. How can we offer ourselves as instruments in a miracle of restoration? Meditate on the text and allow yourself to become one of the disciples in the story. Hear Jesus' words: "Gather up the fragments left over, so that nothing may be lost" (John 6:12). How do they apply to us?

Introduction

When I was a little girl I thought my father could do anything. My father has always been good with his hands, especially in building and repairing things. I used to tell my friends not to worry if they ever had a broken toy because my dad could fix anything. As I grew older, I realized that there were some things my father could not fix. Broken bones, broken dreams, broken relationships, and broken hearts are not fixed by a hammer and nail. I am sure it must be difficult for him to realize that there are things in his child's life that he cannot fix or change. However, his presence, prayers, and love provide the space for healing to occur.

Body

Over the course of my life and ministry, I have come to understand more from my father's perspective. I have people who come to my office whose lives are broken, whose relationships are fragmented, and whose spirits are wounded. They cry about the things that have happened in their lives and all I can do is to provide a presence, offer prayers, and surround them with the love I hope sincerely reflects Jesus' love. The feeding of the five thousand story provides a sense of direction and purpose as to how we are called to live as Jesus' disciples.

Imagine the scene: It's dinnertime, the people are hungry and the disciples are clearly nervous about this crowd. Perhaps they knew that people who are physically discomforted get agitated. They might have feared there would be a riot. Jesus proposes that the disciples buy bread to feed this hungry crowd. The disciples respond by calculating the cost of feeding the crowd. It would be impossible for the disciples to find the money to feed this crowd.

I think the disciples' reaction is very typical. People all around us are experiencing hurt and we don't want them to talk about their pain because it makes us feel uncomfortable. Homeless people sit on our street corners, but it takes only a moment to avert our eyes and walk by them. If we could just send these folks away with all their problems, then we wouldn't have to feel obligated. But Jesus was not going to let the disciples off that easy. He knows that the problem is relatively simple for him, but that it is the source of a great deal of anxiety for them. The people will receive the food they need to be temporarily satisfied. But after the crowd is fed, Jesus and his disciples do not just sit around waiting for someone to clean up. Jesus instructs his disciples, "Gather up the fragments left over, so that nothing may be lost."

Isn't this a strange instruction? Why was Jesus concerned about the leftovers? Perhaps without stretching the text too much, we might find an interesting link between the story as recorded and the audience who may have heard this story in the first century. The intended audience was the early church who was struggling with brokenness and fragmentation. They were persecuted and rejected by their own families. Some had given up on the faith and betrayed other Christians. What would this instruction mean to them?

At the end of the instruction, the word "lost" (*apollumi* in the Greek) means to destroy fully, to perish or lose. It almost seems as if Jesus' instruction is about people rather than food. It is the same word that Jesus uses in John 3:16, where it is translated as perish. "For God so loved the world that he gave his only Son, so that everyone who believes in him may not perish but may have eternal life."

Can we hear something about Jesus' intention for our brokenness? Does Jesus worry about the leftovers? The leftover people who are broken and shattered are important to him and he gives us an instruction to pick up the broken pieces. We can't mend the brokenness, that is God's action, but we can make sure that we are there to be instruments of reconciliation and healing.

Conclusion

When we bring the broken pieces to Jesus, he restores and renews them into a new creation. Sue Bender writes: "I saw a strikingly handsome Japanese tea bowl that had been broken and pieced together. The image of that bowl made a lasting impression. Instead of trying to hide the flaws, the cracks were emphasized—filled with silver. The bowl was even more precious after it had been mended" (*Everyday Sacred,* Harper San Francisco, p. 13).

God uses our brokenness so that something more precious can be created. All God asks of us is to gather the broken ones so that none may be lost.

NOTES

Paid in Full

Ordinary Time

(15 min.)   **Pastor:** Introduction to the service

WL: Lead Call to Worship.
1. "I Am Not My Own" (Nystrom) SB#6, 491
2. "I'm So Glad" (unknown) SB#6, 495
3. "Sing and Be Glad in Him" (DeShazo) SB#6, 525
4. "I Will Worship You, Lord" (Gardner) SFPW, 21

WL: Read prayer as introduction to the next song.
5. "I Come to the Cross" (Somma & Batstone) PHC, 122

WL: Ask the ushers to receive the offering.
6. "Jesus, Draw Me Close" (Founds) PHC, 209

Solo: "He Covers Me" as performed by Steve Camp from *Doin' My Best Vol. 1* (Sparrow Records); or "Amazing Grace" (UMH, 378)

(25 min.)   **Pastor:** Sermon
Segment #1: No Debt
Segment #2: Canceled Debt
Segment #3: Forgiven Debt

Movie Clip: *The Color Purple* (Warner Brothers)
Description: Shug is singing at Harpo's place while her father is preaching at the church across the river.
Start Time: 2:19:10
Start Cue: Harpo is letting down the drawbridge to let people across to his club.
End Time: 2:23:40
End Cue: Shug and her father embrace. Shug says, "See, Daddy, sinners have a song, too." Camera shot on Celia and Sophia's faces.

Segment #4: Your Debt
Have the scripture presentation with interpretive dance (Luke 7:37-50). As background music for the dancer, use "Woman in the Night" (UMH, 274). At the   conclusion of the scripture, have a soloist sing stanza 4 of the hymn while the dancer continues.

(15 min.)   **Pastor:** Lead a congregational prayer time, followed by an invitation for the people to come forward to have the backs of their hands stamped with the word "PAID." Quiet reflective music should be played during this time.

PT singers should come forward first during the time of reflection and then prepare to lead the closing song
7. "He Whom the Son Sets Free" (Nystrom) SB#6, 483

Pastor: Lead the Benediction by saying, "Repeat after me" *(see Benediction)*.

Music Sources: *Praise Worship Songbook #6* (Integrity); *Praise Hymns and Choruses, 4th ed.* (Maranatha); *Songs for Praise & Worship* (Word); *The United Methodist Hymnal* (UMPH)

INTRODUCTION TO THE SERVICE

I don't know what type of burdens you have brought to this service. Some of you have come with heavy debts. Those debts may be financial, personal, or spiritual. Whatever type they are, before you leave you can know that those debts have been paid in full.

CALL TO WORSHIP

L: Jesus knows his people.
P: Jesus knows my inner thoughts.
L: Jesus has the authority to forgive sins.
P: Jesus has forgiven my sins.
L: Let us praise Jesus for his sacrifice, which was payment for all our sins. We are truly a free people.

PRAYER

Forgiving God, sometimes it is hard to believe that we can be free from all that burdens us. Yet, you have promised us that we can have true freedom in you. We claim that freedom as we prepare our hearts to hear your Word. Help us to be drawn into your presence by your grace. Amen.

SCRIPTURE PRESENTATION (Luke 7:37-50)

Characters: Jesus, Simon, and Woman in costume; Narrator (reads scripture from the back of the room)

1. Jesus and Simon enter and are seated at an imaginary table (v. 36).
2. Woman enters, walking dejectedly, with a jar of ointment (v. 37).
3. Woman leans over Jesus' feet pretending to wipe them, place ointment on them, and kiss them (v. 38).
4. Woman continues to kiss Jesus' feet (v. 39).
5. Woman interprets story with dance movements (vv. 40-48).
6. Narrator (v. 49).
7. Woman begins dance to stanza 4 of "Woman in the Night" (*sing refrain twice*) (v. 50).

BENEDICTION

I have no debt. (*Repeat.*)
My debt is cancelled. (*Repeat.*)
Jesus has forgiven *all* my debt. (*Repeat.*)
I am paid in full! (*Repeat.*)

ALTAR

White silklike fabric is draped on the front of the altar with a similar weight teal fabric draped on the top and down the sides. A large blue bowl with a white pillar candle stands in the middle. Three small blue votive candles are in front. There is a pitcher, basin, and towel on the right side, several goblets in different sizes and styles across the top of the altar, and a bowl of grapes on the left side—all representative of the scripture.

OPTIONS

Music ♫

"All We Like Sheep" (Moen) *Come & Worship* (Integrity)
"Amazing Love" (Kendrick) *Come & Worship* (Integrity)
"Hide Me in Your Holiness" (Ragsdale) *Praise Hymns & Choruses (4th ed.)* (Maranatha)
"I Need You" (Founds) *Praise Hymns & Choruses (4th ed.)* (Maranatha)

Recordings

"He Is All You Need" as performed by Steve Camp, from *Doin' My Best, Vol. 1* (Sparrow Records)
"He'll Never Let You Go" as performed by Phillips, Craig and Dean, from *Phillips, Craig and Dean* (Star Song Records)

Drama

Sinbusters by Dave McClellan, Cross Point Script #13620. (*See introduction for resource.*)
Characters: Narrator; Sinbuster #1 and #2; Man; Counselor; Counselee
Time: 5-6 minutes
Purpose: The sin problem has been around a long time and it seems there are two basic approaches Christians take to deal with the problem. The first is to condemn and alienate all who make the fatal mistake of revealing their less-than-distinguished side. The other is to overlook and downplay the seriousness of sin. This sketch seeks a more balanced approach.

SERMON

Idea Generator

Did you know that in 1997 installment credit had grown to over 1 trillion dollars? From March 1997 to March 1998, over 1.3 million people filed for personal bankruptcy. The causes of financial problems include excessive use of credit, reduced income through loss of job, poor money management, and divorce. Suddenly the excessive amount of debt seems more than a financial problem. The desire to accumulate possessions more than the desire to live in God's plans, loss of a job, divorce or separation are each indications of spiritual crisis points. There is a very good chance that someone sitting in your congregation is dealing with a heavy financial debt. There is also a good chance that someone in your congregation has a deep spiritual problem arising out of that debt.

"Our debt has been paid by Jesus" is a loaded statement for many people. It has been used by some to institute a response of guilt rather than gratefulness for God's graciousness. The preacher has a challenge to access the language of the culture concerning debt and reclaim it for the church.

As a spiritual exercise, use the Internet or your local library to acquaint yourself with the crisis of debt in our country. It will help you pastor the people whom you serve. There are faces that make up these statistics.

Introduction

Debt is a four-letter word. In many ways, the word provokes a variety of emotions. For the person who is in serious financial debt, it can be a source of health problems, anxiety, and embarrassment. It is one of the taboo subjects in church. It's OK to say that you have lost your job and ask for prayer. But no one wants to ask for prayer because they have an overwhelming amount of credit card debt.

At most parties, people feel free to talk about very personal health problems. However, let someone start to talk about going through bankruptcy and there is an uncomfortable silence. I believe that is because most of us are in some sort of financial debt. We are living from paycheck to paycheck regardless of our income. It really makes us uncomfortable when someone volunteers unsolicited information about personal financial problems.

In the scripture text, Jesus is eating with a man named Simon. In the middle of the meal, a woman who is known for her sinful lifestyle enters the house and washes Jesus' feet with her tears. She also anoints Jesus' feet with a costly ointment. Simon is appalled and embarrassed. People's willingness to admit their powerlessness and need for relief makes us uncomfortable. It causes us to look inside our own pocketbook or in Simon's case, inside his own heart.

Body

Segment #1: No Debt

Often when people find they are in debt, they will seek the help of a consumer credit counselor. The first thing the counselor will tell them is to cut up all their credit cards. This is one of the hardest actions for a person who has accumulated a great deal of debt. It is too easy to get a credit card. Many people have been using credit cards to borrow from one in order to pay another. It has become a vicious cycle. The counselor recognizes that the cycle must be stopped at the point of the problem! *(At this point the pastor holds up a credit card and scissors and declares that everyone will get to the root of their debt problem today. The credit card is cut in half.)* Cutting the credit card in half stops the person in debt from spending. But this is only the first step to freedom. The accumulated credit card debt must be paid back.

In the Jewish tradition, there was a custom called the Sabbatical Year. "Every seventh year you shall grant a remission of debts" (Deut. 15:1). Wouldn't it be great if we still observed that custom in our tradition? But the reality for us is that our debts have to be paid.

Segment #2: Canceled Debt

There is no custom in our time in which debts are wiped clean. Yet sometimes we experience just a little taste of grace by those to whom we are indebted on a larger scale simply because of their love for us.

A little boy decided that he wanted to give his mother a bill for all the chores he had done around the house. While he was at school, his mother found a piece of paper on the kitchen counter with these words:

Mowing lawn	$2.00
Taking out the trash	$1.00
Cleaning room	$2.50
Total	$5.50

When the boy arrived home, he found a bill from his mother on his bed:

Sewing patches on Boy Scout uniform
Paid in Full
Taking forgotten homework to school
Paid in Full
Putting up tent for backyard sleepover
Paid in Full
Staying up all night when you were sick
Paid in Full

Like this little boy, we tally up what we think we are owed. In our spiritual lives, we look at how much time, energy, and money we give to the church. We begin to tally up our bill for God. And yet our work is so insignificant compared to what God has done for us. God cancels our debt.

Segment #3: Forgiven Debt

In the story of the prodigal son, the son experiences firsthand the relief of being welcomed back into his family after squandering his half of the inheritance. He was ready to go back home and take his chances on working off this debt as a slave, but he was surprised by the extravagance of his father's love. His father's reaction to his homecoming screams "forgiven" more loudly than the spoken acknowledgment. In the movie, *The Color Purple,* Shug has been estranged from her preacher father for many years. But through the music of their faith, they are able to reach out to each other in reconciliation and forgiveness. (*Show movie clip; see script for details.*)

Segment #4: Your Debt

The word *indebted* means to be legally or morally obligated in some way. We have all made mistakes. We all wish we could somehow erase some incidents from our past. Maybe some of us are living out the circumstances of our past or present. That is a debt just as surely as the debt on our credit cards. The difference is that this debt can be expunged or wiped out by Jesus' love. The slate of our heart can be wiped clean. Jesus not only forgave our debt but also decided he would make the payment for us. Our debt is not only forgiven, it is paid in full. (*Perform scripture presentation with interpretive dance. See script.*)

NOTES _____

_____

_____

_____

_____

_____

_____

_____

_____

_____

_____

_____

_____

Receiving Our Commission

(15 min.)   **Call to Worship Skit:** *Time Warp to Pentecost*

Scripture Reading: Acts 2:1-21

PT: Lead the opening songs.
1. "Let Your Spirit Rise Within Me" (Speir) SFPW, 235
2. "The Spirit of the Lord" (Funk) C&W, 168
3. "Spirit of the Living God" (Iverson) SFPW, 131
4. "Holy Spirit, Thou Art Welcome" (Rambo/Huntsinger) SFPW, 133

(15 min.)   **Pastor:** Lead congregational prayer time.

5. "Sweet, Sweet Spirit" (Akers) SFPW, 136
6. "You Are" (Graham/Townley) CC, 53
7. "Surely the Presence" (Wolfe) CCB, 1

Special music with interpretive dance: "Spirit Blow Through Me" (Mott/Eller/Ivory), Big 3 Music from *New Hope Praise Band: They That Wait on the Lord*

(20 min.)   **Pastor:** Sermon

(10 min.)   **Response to the Word** *(See sermon notes.)*

PT: Lead the closing song.
8. "Catch the Spirit" (Zabel) CC, 56

Pastor or WL: Benediction

Music Sources: *Songs for Praise & Worship* (Word); *Come Celebrate!* (Abingdon Press); *Come & Worship* (Integrity)

CALL TO WORSHIP SKIT: *Time Warp to Pentecost*

Characters: Captain of a starship *(a strong voice heard offstage)*; two starship officers

(Play the soundtrack music of Star Trek or other space themes as background music while the Captain is reading the introduction.)

Captain: Space, the final frontier. These are the voyages of the starship *Enterprise*. Its mission: To explore strange new worlds, to seek out new life and new civilizations, to boldly go where no one has gone before.

(Two starship officers enter, one with a communication device.)

Officer: Captain, it appears that we have gone through a time warp. Our preliminary estimates place us in Jerusalem in the year A.D. 35.

Captain: Can you describe what is happening?

Officer: It appears that there is some sort of commotion. A large group of people has gathered. They all seem to be speaking different languages. There is one group of people who are quite agitated. This could turn into a riot. Wait! Someone is addressing the crowd. The man giving the message is talking about Jesus.

Captain: I believe that you have arrived at Pentecost.

Officer: Pentecost?

Captain: Beam up and we'll access it on the computer. *(Pause as the two officers exit.)* Here it is. The history is located in the book of Acts, chapter 2, verses 1 to 21. It reads . . . *(Read the scripture.)*

BENEDICTION

Our mission is the world. Let us go boldly to proclaim the gospel. Hallelujah, Amen! *(Alternative: Recite your mission statement.)*

ALTAR

A large gold traditional cross with a dove attached is in the center of the altar. Fourteen red candles of various sizes and shapes cover the altar. Silk ivy is used as filler. Red tulle drapes the top and the sides of the altar to the floor. White tulle is laid on top of the red tulle. The candles for the congregation to light can be placed in a basket on the small table in front of the altar (left side).

OPTIONS

Music

"Anointing Fall on Me" (Thomas) *Come Celebrate!* (Abingdon Press)
"Come, Holy Spirit" (Gaither) *Songs for Praise & Worship* (Word)
"Spirit Blowing Through Creation" (Haugen) *Come Celebrate!* (Abingdon Press)
"Spirit of God" (Ross/Till) *Songs for Praise & Worship* (Word)
"Spirit Song" (Wimber) *Come Celebrate!* (Abingdon Press)
"Wind of the Spirit" (Hanson/Murakami) *Come Celebrate!* (Abingdon Press)

Recordings

"Be the One" as performed by Al Denson, from *Be the One* (Benson Records)
"The Message" as performed by 4 Him, from *The Message* (Benson Records)

SERMON

Idea Generator

In reading the story of Pentecost found in the second chapter of Acts, it is easy to let one's imagination focus on the obvious miraculous images. Wind, fire, and speaking in strange languages offer the opportunity to create a wild and striking worship service. But what pastor would not yearn to experience the lasting miracle of Pentecost in his or her own church? The lasting miracle of Pentecost is the changed heart and determination of the disciples. The disciples were no longer a scared little band of people whose leader had somehow left the scene. They were now an emboldened group of dynamic, charismatic explorers for Jesus. They had a mission and they had no doubt about what it was.

Imagine for a moment what would happen in the church, community, and world if that same miracle occurred in your service today. With special effects, we can recreate fire and wind. Anyone who has ever ridden an amusement park ride knows we can reproduce some of the same experiences, but only the Holy Spirit can give us meaning and purpose. Only the Holy Spirit can fill us with boldness to be change agents to the entire world. This is where we will see the real miracles take place.

Would it not be a wonderful spiritual exercise for the pastor and praise team to spend special time in preparation together this week in their own upper room? That's how it started.

Introduction

"Space, the final frontier. These are the voyages of the starship *Enterprise*. Its mission: To explore strange new worlds, to seek out new life and new civilizations, to boldly go where no one has gone before." This was the opening speech of Captain James T. Kirk and Captain Jean Luc Picard as an introduction to the continuing voyage and mission of the starship *Enterprise*.

Nearly two thousand years before, when Luke wrote the Acts of the Apostles, he could have given us a similar statement concerning the mission of the spirit-filled disciples. Maybe it would be something like this: The World. These are the acts of the disciples of Jesus. Their mission: To be witnesses to the ends of earth. To go boldly where no one has ever proclaimed the gospel and to be bearers of Good News.

Body

Jesus has ascended into heaven and the disciples have returned to Jerusalem and are waiting for some promised sign about their next step. The second chapter of Acts opens with an exciting and mind-boggling special effects sequence. Wind and fire, symbols of God's presence, provide a sensory experience, but the description of that moment is only found in the first four verses of the second chapter of Acts. The real miracle is the one that cannot be seen but will be felt by the whole world for all time. The real miracle is that this ragtag band of fishermen, tax collectors, and women would be transformed into the nucleus of a movement that would influence and affect the entire earth.

Remember this is the group of people who argued about their own greatness. This is the same group of people who deserted Jesus at the first sign of trouble. They ran and hid, afraid of being associated with this radical movement. One of them even become intimidated by a servant girl's question and denied any knowledge of a relationship with Jesus. Suddenly, this same group will preach and teach in every place they find themselves. They will face jail and persecution without fear. They will go boldly where before they had been afraid. They became secure in their mission.

The real miracle of Pentecost is what happened after that day and what is continuing to happen because of the Holy Spirit's life-changing empowerment of these disciples.

The disciples had no doubt about their mission. God had created them for this purpose. Jesus had taught and commissioned them and the Holy Spirit had authorized and equipped them. They were ready to begin this adventure, taking off as if they were moving to warp speed. Nothing could stop them. Thousands upon thousands were converted. The church grew despite opposition and persecution. In every town and community they proclaimed the Good News.

Conclusion

What would we see if the real miracle of Pentecost happened here in this place? What if you left here assured of your mission as a disciple of Christ? As a church we have developed a mission statement. *(If your church does not have a mission statement, this might be a great opportunity to encourage church members to begin the discernment process to develop one.)* How does the mission statement make a difference in how we develop our ministries?

The people on the starship *Enterprise* knew the mission in which they had been commissioned. Usually at some point during an episode the crew was reminded in some way of their mission. It gave them meaning and purpose. The mission drove the series, because without a mission, what would be the purpose of following the adventure?

Perhaps we have experienced a lack of enthusiasm throughout the world because the church universal has forgotten its mission. It is the same as that of the band of disciples in the upper room: "Go therefore and make disciples of all nations, baptizing them in the name of the Father and of the Son and of the Holy Spirit, and teaching them to obey everything that I have commanded you. And remember, I am with you always, to the end of the age" (Matt. 28:19-20).

RESPONSE TO THE WORD

Pentecost is often called the birthday of the Church. On birthdays, there is usually a cake and the birthday boy or girl makes a wish and blows out the candles. Today on our altar we have candles representing God's power and the empowerment of God's commissioned people. As a response to the Word, you may come forward and receive a candle. Instead of blowing out candles, we are going to light our candles as a symbol of our own empowerment by God's spirit. At this time you will also be given a reminder of our mission (see below). Place it somewhere in your home and remember your mission.

(Print your church's mission statement on a business-size card that has an attached magnet. This is an inexpensive way to advertise your church's mission. While the people are coming forward to light their candle and receive a magnet, play background music and your own mission video, if you use video projection.)

Video Suggestion: Ask someone in your congregation to videotape people who visually depict your church's mission statement. This could include visiting at a hospital, serving at a soup kitchen, a Bible study, a worship service, or children's Sunday school.

NOTES _____

_____

_____

_____

_____

_____

_____

_____

_____

_____

_____

_____

_____

_____

_____

_____

_____

_____

_____

The Jesus Files

Ascension Sunday

(5 min.)   **Call to Worship Skit:** *The Investigation*
1. "Lord, I Lift Your Name on High" (Founds) CCB, 36
2. "Sing and Be Glad in Him" (DeShazo) SB#6, 525
3. "Awesome God" (Mullins) SFPW, 11

(15 min.)   **Mulder** and **Scully** enter to begin interviewing people in the congregation. Prearrange for certain people to be able to give answers to any of the questions.
(Play The X-Files *theme at the beginning and end of each interview.)*

Interview #1: What evidence do you have that this Jesus really exists?
4. "Because He Lives" (Gaither) SFPW, 123
5. "I Live" (Cook) SFPW, 124

Interview #2: Tell me what you know about this Jesus.
6. "Great Is the Lord Almighty!" (Jernigan) SFPW, 58

Interview #3: Why do you believe Jesus is alive today?
7. "For This Purpose" (Kendrick) SFPW, 125

(10 min.)   **WL:** Lead Affirmation of Faith and prayer.
8. "Open Our Eyes, Lord" (Cull) SFPW, 199

Pastor: Lead a congregational prayer time by asking for a few responses to the question, "Where have you seen Jesus?" Conclude with the Lord's Prayer.

(15 min.)   **Pastor:** Report of Findings *(See sermon notes.)*
(Play videotape of The Visual Bible *or read the scripture—Acts 1:1-12.)*

Pastor: Final Report: Show the question, "How will *you* be a witness?"
(See sermon notes.)

(10 min.)   Receive the offering while the band plays "Carry the Light."
(Ask the congregation to stand and greet one another and tell someone what they have witnessed about Jesus this week.)

PT: Lead the closing song.
9. "Carry the Light" (Paris) SFPW, 143

Mulder and Scully: Benediction

Music Sources: *Songs for Praise & Worship* (Word); *Cokesbury Chorus Book* (Abingdon Press); *Praise Worship Songbook #6* (Integrity)

CALL TO WORSHIP SKIT: *The Investigation*

*(Two FBI agents, **Mulder** [man] and **Scully** [woman] enter.)*

Mulder: We've got a case over at [Name] Church. There have been some really strange happenings.

Scully: What kind of strange happenings?

Mulder: People are getting together every week to do some really strange things.

Scully: What kind of strange things?

Mulder: To begin with, they read a book about a guy they call Jesus. Get this, after this Jesus guy dies, they say he rose from the dead and they even say they have a personal relationship with him. And would you believe . . . ?

Scully: *(Interrupting)* Wait a minute. I believe that would certainly qualify as a strange phenomenon.

Mulder: I believe this investigation needs to be a top priority. Where should we start?

Scully: Well, where do you think?

(Both exit.)

AFFIRMATION OF FAITH

We believe in Jesus. We believe that Jesus died and was raised from the dead. We believe that Jesus is known through his word, his creation, his people, and his love.

PRAYER

Awesome God, we give you thanks that through your word, your creation, your people and your love, we have the evidence we need to help us believe. In the times where evidence is not perceived or understood, we know without a doubt that our faith is solid because faith is the substance of things hoped for and the evidence of things not seen. Amen.

BENEDICTION

(Mulder and Scully enter.)

Mulder: I think that the people we interviewed really believe.

Scully: It certainly appears that way.

Mulder: What about you, do you believe?

Scully: Of course. With this much evidence, how can I not believe?

ALTAR

A white cloth covers the altar. Ten yards of teal polyester is draped on top of the altar and down the right side. White tulle covers this fabric to give it a heavenly effect for Ascension Sunday. A silk fern is on each corner of the altar. A gold triangle (cardboard covered with gold ribbon) is in the center with a white pillar candle on a gold holder behind the triangle.

OPTIONS

Music

"In Him We Live" (Speir) *Songs for Praise & Worship* (Word)

"Jesus Is King" (Churchill) *Songs for Praise & Worship* (Word)

"Lord, I Believe In You" (Walker) *Praise Hymns & Choruses (4th ed.)* (Maranatha)

"The Lord Is My Light" (Nelson) *Songs for Praise & Worship* (Word)

"This Is What I Believe" (Schreiner & Harrah) *Praise Hymns & Choruses (4th ed.)* (Maranatha)

"We Declare That the Kingdom of God Is Here" (Kendrick) *Come & Worship* (Integrity)

Recordings

"The Victor" as performed by Steve Green, from *The Mission* (Sparrow Records)

"Jesus Is Alive" as performed by Ron Kenoly, from *Jesus Is Alive* (Hosanna!/Integrity Records)

SERMON

Idea Generator

There are times in the cycle of life when people try to make meaning out of the mysteries of life. The pop culture of the 1990s has definitely been an indication that we are in this cycle. Movies about interaction with other life forms, such as *Contact* and *Men in Black,* push us to think of our significance in the universe. Music that has an otherworldly, mysterious quality is at the top of the charts. Even the famous and acclaimed of our society have latched on to the spirituality craze. As we've entered into the year 2000, this cycle is heightened by advanced computer systems, virtual reality games, and what seems like science fictional advances in medicine.

Take a survey of pop culture this week. What are the popular television shows, movies, and books? During the time of this writing, *The X-Files* was a popular television show. The struggle of two FBI agents to make sense of unexplainable phenomenon has become a metaphor for many of the struggles in our own lives. Is there something outside of ourselves? What evidence is there that our relationship with Jesus is real?

Most people really want to believe. The church is in a prime position to proclaim what we know to be truth. Jesus is alive! We can know and be in a relationship with Jesus.

Introduction

For most of us, there is a deep need to believe that there is something in the universe that is outside of ourselves. We are fascinated with science fiction. We toy with the idea of life beyond the grave. We flock to places where something miraculous has occurred. And yet, while we need to believe, many of us have trouble because we also want to be able to understand logically the world around us. We want evidence.

Our two investigators have pushed us on three points. What evidence do you have that this Jesus really exists? Tell me what you know about this Jesus. Why do you believe Jesus is alive today?

Body

(This service is designed for the preacher and worship team to integrate the congregation's responses as the point of the sermon. While your congregation will be different from others, I am sure there will be common elements that are found in all congregations.)

Some people claim that Jesus exists because in times of crisis or tragedy they have experienced and known the presence of Jesus. In the death of a loved one, waiting for the results of medical tests, in times of financial crisis, the community of faith has surrounded them as a testimony that Jesus exists.

When their hearts could not sing, the community sang for them. When they could not pay their electric bill, the community shared from their resources. When they faced chemotherapy, the community cared for their children.

Jesus exists as evidenced through those who bear his name as Christian. We are the evidence of the presence of Christ because we choose the path of self-giving, which is not instinctual to our corrupt human nature. We choose that path because we are one in alliance with the Almighty who loves through us when we are incapable of loving.

The investigators asked us to describe what we know about this Jesus. We know Jesus through his life story found in the Word of God, the Bible. This is our Jesus Files. We know he loves people just as they are. Jesus ate and fellowshiped with those on the margins of society. Listen to his own words: "The Spirit of the Lord is upon me, because he has anointed me to bring good news to the poor. He has sent me to proclaim release to the captives and recovery of sight to the blind, to let the oppressed go free. To proclaim the year of the Lord's favor" (Luke 4:18-19).

We also know Jesus through the demonstration of his love by the community of faith as described above. Name the ways you have seen his love realized in your own life.

Why do we believe Jesus is alive today? That is the essential question to which every believer must be able to give a ready answer. If Jesus were just a great teacher who lived and died two thousand years ago, then the community of faith has no purpose. We can help one another and fellowship in any social or civic group. But if Jesus is the Son of God, who died and came back from the dead, then we have no choice but to proclaim this incredible news to everyone. Why do we believe Jesus is alive today? What is your answer?

Conclusion

The Final Report

People are desperate for the truth. The tag line that ends the weekly episodes of *The X-Files* is "The truth is out there." Christians know the truth. It is not out there somewhere, it is inside our hearts. You might not have had the chance to verbally answer the questions posed by our investigators, but my hope is that you have answered the questions with the truth of your relationship with Jesus.

When Jesus ascended into heaven, two men suddenly appeared and said to the disciples, "Why do you stand looking up toward heaven? This Jesus, who has been taken up from you into heaven, will come in the same way as you saw him go to heaven" (Acts 1:11). The disciples could not just keep standing there with mouths open and an awestruck look in their eyes. It was time to witness. Do you believe Jesus is alive today? Share the truth.

NOTES _____

_____

_____

_____

_____

_____

_____

_____

Can I Have a Witness?

Communion

(10 min.) **Call to Worship Skit:** *Let Me Tell You*

Solo: "Witness" (Traditional Spiritual)
(The soloist should walk from the back of the room to the front while singing.)

WL: Lead the unison prayer of confession.
　　1. "Shine, Jesus, Shine" (Kendrick) PHC, 238
　　2. "Be Bold, Be Strong" (Chapman) SFPW, 207
　　3. "Stand Up" (Carroll) PHC, 240

WL: Give a short introduction to the next two songs.
　　4. "We Will Glorify" (Paris) SFPW, 68
　　5. "Christ in Us Be Glorified" (Chapman) PHC, 176

(10 min.) **Pastor:** Pastoral prayer
　　6. "Step by Step" (Beaker) CC, 63

Solo or recording: "The Message" as performed by 4 Him, from *The Message* (Benson Records)

(20 min.) **Pastor:** Sermon

(5 min.) **Faith Witness:** Ask a congregational member to give a witness.

(10 min.) **Pastor:** Consecrate the communion elements.
During communion use the song "People Need the Lord" (Nelson/McHugh) as a solo, anthem, or recording. Offerings may be brought forward.

Solo: Like the beginning of the service, the soloist should exit singing "Witness" (Traditional Spiritual) and encourage the congregation to join in singing.

Pastor or WL: Benediction

Music Sources: *Praise Hymns and Choruses, 4th ed.* (Maranatha); *Songs for Praise & Worship* (Word); *Cokesbury Chorus Book* (Abingdon Press)

CALL TO WORSHIP SKIT: *Let Me Tell You*

WL#1: *(To WL#2)* You know, I sure hope this service will be over quickly. I didn't have time for breakfast and I am *so* hungry. I just know my stomach is going to start growling at an inappropriate time. I wonder where we should go to eat today?

WL#2: Well, let me tell you about this fantastic new restaurant that I tried the other day. I had to wait in line a while but was it ever worth it! The food was out of this world. The four of us who went each ordered something different so we could taste as many things as possible. Each dish was superb. I give this imported chef an A+. You've got to try it. I promise you'll love it. Trust me!

WL#1: Of course I trust you. How can I *not* try it since you are so enthusiastic!

(Both freeze.)

Pastor: Are you just as enthusiastic about your faith?

PRAYER OF CONFESSION

Gracious God, you have called us to be your witnesses, but are we able? We confess that we become entrapped in the glitter and glitz of society and our desires become self-centered. Our witness becomes tarnished. We pray, O God, for your Holy Spirit to breathe into us enthusiasm, truth, and witness. We desire our witness to be polished by the Holy Spirit so that we may reflect your story. Amen.

BENEDICTION

Pastor: Will you be a witness for our Lord?
People: Yes, I will be a witness for our Lord.
All: Hallelujah, Amen!

ALTAR

Teal fabric is draped on top of the white altar cloth. A traditional gold cross is in the center with the communion elements in front of the cross. An asparagus fern is on the left side. The triple iron candelabra is on the right side with an arrangement of silk ivy, hydrangea, and grapes in front of it.

OPTIONS

Music 🎵
"Carry the Light" (Paris) *Songs for Praise & Worship* (Word)
"Freely, Freely" (Owens) *The United Methodist Hymnal* (UMPH)
"Here I Am, Lord" (Schutte) *The United Methodist Hymnal* (UMPH)
"Send Me" (Graves) *Praise Hymns & Choruses, 4th ed.* (Maranatha)
"Song for the Nations" (Christensen) *Songs for Praise & Worship* (Word)
"Tell the World" (Skidmore) *Praise Hymns & Choruses, 4th ed.* (Maranatha)

Recordings 📼
"A Lot Like You" as performed by 4 Him, from *The Message* (Benson Records)
"Be the One" as performed by Al Denson, from *Be the One* (Benson Records)
"Center of the Mark" as performed by 4 Him, from *The Message* (Benson Records)

SERMON

Idea Generator

In many recent conversations with colleagues, I hear the same frustrations. The basic concern is how to help people move from the place of receiving ministry to the place of being in ministry. It is our challenge and mandate as the body of Christ to do so. However, for many people, what occurs on Sunday morning never really affects how they are in relationship with others during the week.

As a spiritual exercise this week ask several people the question, "What is your ministry?" For some the answer might be serving on committees and administrating the business of the church. But there is a difference between administration and ministry. Even pastors and church leaders get confused about this. If asked, how would you define the difference? What is ministry? What is *your* ministry?

Introduction

The first-century church existed in a hostile environment. Christianity was considered one of many choices in a diverse religious culture. Christianity was not ever considered an obvious choice. In this environment there was an increasing gap between the have and have-nots. Life was cheap and it was not unusual for children or the elderly to be looked upon as dispensable.

The culture in which we live has many similarities to the first-century culture that existed when Christianity was born. Yet, the early church converted thousands upon thousands. We read in Acts of mass conversions and powerful faith stories. If we exist in a culture much like the first-century church, why are we not making an impact upon the world in much the same way? Has Christianity run its course? I don't think so. Perhaps the reason the church is not making a significant impact on the world is that, unlike the early Christians; we lack focus and purpose.

The first-century church received their mandate from Jesus for their purpose and ministry: "But you will receive power when the Holy Spirit has come upon you; and you will be my witnesses in Jerusalem, in all Judea and Samaria, and to the ends of the earth" (Acts 1:8). There is no mistaking what the mission of the early church was because we are the evidence of their witness. The early church claimed the ministry assigned to them by Jesus. They were to be witnesses.

Something has happened over the last two thousand years. We have forsaken the ministry of witness for the task of administrating. Someone has described this as the difference between being fishers of men and women versus being keepers of the aquarium. That is a great analogy. We have become too concerned with maintenance rather than with witnessing.

Perhaps we sometimes stereotype what witnessing for Jesus means or how a witness approaches the task. Let's examine that more fully by looking at three elements involved in the task of witnessing.

Body

I. Know It.

Do you have a faith story? Could you tell your faith story? The apostle Peter reminds us to "Always be ready to make your defense to anyone who demands from you an accounting for the hope that is in you" (1 Pet. 3:15). Your story is your story. Only you know how your relationship with Jesus was born and how it has grown. If you haven't really thought about your faith story, write it down. Putting it on paper will be a spiritual exercise that will affirm who you are as a child of God. But that is not all. Not only do you have to know your story in order to witness, you also have to grow your story.

II. Grow It.

My friend who is an accomplished pianist must practice regularly to keep her skills sharp. Our faith is not something that happens at a definite point in time and then that is the end of the story. We are on a journey and if we intend to develop into the people we are called to be, we have to take responsibility for growing our faith.

I have often thought that I feel like a sitter in the church nursery. Many people remain babies in the faith. It is a choice, because growing one's faith does not happen automatically. "For though, by this time you ought to be teachers, you need someone to teach you again the basic elements of the oracles of God. You need milk, not solid food; for everyone who lives on milk, being still an infant, is unskilled in the word of righteousness. But solid food is for the mature, for those whose faculties have been trained by practice to distinguish good from evil" (Heb. 5:12-14).

III. Show It.

The final step to being a witness is to show and share with others. There has been a popular saying among Christians in recent years: "What would Jesus do?" By reading scripture, we can understand clearly how Jesus responds in a given situation. The larger question is: "What do you who claim to follow Jesus do?" Of course that would be a little difficult to capture on a bracelet or bumper sticker. The important thing is that it is captured in our hearts. How do you show the personal story that you know and that you are growing?

"I pray that the sharing of your faith may become effective when you perceive all the good that we may do for Christ" (Philemon 6).

Music Resources

The following is a list of the music books (with abbreviations) used to reference songs for the worship services.

CC   Townley, Cathy and Mike Graham, eds. *Come Celebrate! Music for Contemporary Worship.* Nashville: Abingdon Press, 1995. Call: 1-800-672-1789.

CCB   *Cokesbury Chorus Book: Praise and Worship Music for Today's Church, Expanded Edition.* Nashville: Abingdon Press, 1999. Call: 1-800-672-1789.

C&W   *Come & Worship: A Collection of 200 Popular Songs for Praise and Worship.* Mobile, Ala.: Integrity Music, Inc., 1994. Call: 1-334-633-9000.

PHC   *Praise Hymns and Choruses, Expanded 4th ed.* Laguna Hills, Calif.: Maranatha! Music, 1997. Call: 1-800-444-4012. Fax: 1-800-245-7664.

SB#6   *Praise Worship: Songbook 6.* Mobile, Ala.: Integrity Music, Inc., 1992. Call: 1-334-633-9000.

SB#9   *Praise Worship: Songbook 9.* Mobile, Ala.: Integrity Music, Inc., 1995. Call: 1-334-633-9000.

TCH   *The Celebration Hymnal: Songs and Hymns for Worship.* Nashville: Word Music/Integrity Music, 1997.

UMH   *The United Methodist Hymnal.* Nashville: The United Methodist Publishing House, 1989. Call: 1-800-672-1789.

SFPW   *Songs for Praise and Worship.* Nashville: Word Music, 1992. Call: 1-888-324-9673.

BOW   *The United Methodist Book of Worship.* The United Methodist Publishing House, 1992. Call: 1-800-672-1789.

Internet Resources for Preaching

Bible in Nine Languages and Multiple Bible Versions
www.bible.gospelcom.net

Christian Spirituality Resources
www.gtu.edu/library/LibSpirit.html

Sermons On Line
www.sermoncentral.com

Sermon Illustrations
www.sermonillustrations.com

Sermon and Commentaries
www.rockies.net/~spirit/sermon.html

News Reports from Various Christian and Secular Resources
www.zondervan.com/newslink.html

Homiletics Magazine—Published by Communication Resources
www.HomileticsOnline.com

The Living Pulpit Magazine
www.pulpit.org

Index of Songs

Title	Composer	Resource
Ah, Lord God	Kay Chance	SFPW, 2
Amazing Love	Graham Kendrick	TCH, 351
Angels from the Realms of Glory	Montgomery/Smart	UMH, 220
Angels We Have Heard on High	(Traditional)	CC, 29
Antiphonal Praise	Steve Green	SFPW, 25
Arise and Sing	Mel Ray, Jr.	SFPW, 225
Arise, Shine	Gary Alan Smith	CCB, 2
At This Time of Giving	Graham Kendrick	Make Way Music
Awesome God	Rich Mullins	SFPW, 11
Awesome Power	John G. Elliott	SFPW, 10
Baptized in Water	Saward/Traditional	TCH, 465
Be Bold, Be Strong	Morris Chapman	SFPW, 207
Be Still and Know	(Anonymous)	SFPW, 49
Because He Lives	William & Gloria Gaither	SFPW, 123
Behold, What Manner of Love	Patricia Van Tine	SFPW, 48
Blessed Be the Name	Don Moen	SFPW, 80
Carry the Light	Twila Paris	SFPW, 143
Catch the Spirit	Lyndy Zabel	CC, 56
Christ in Us Be Glorified	Morris Chapman	PHC, 176
Christ the Lord Is Risen Today	Charles Wesley	CC, 48
Come and Behold Him	Chisum/Searcy	SB#9, 722
Come into the King's Chambers	Daniel Gardner	SFPW, 24
Come to the Table	Cloninger/Nystrom	SB#6, 471
Fill My Cup, Lord	Richard Blanchard	CCB, 47
For This Purpose	Graham Kendrick	SFPW, 125
Glorify Thy Name	Donna Adkins	SFPW, 19
Good Christian Friends, Rejoice	(Traditional)	CC, 27
Great Is the Lord Almighty!	Dennis Jernigan	SFPW, 58
Hallowed Be Thy Name	Mason/Lawson	SFPW, 41
Hark! the Herald Angels Sing	Wesley/Mendelssohn	CC, 30
He Is Exalted	Twila Paris	SFPW, 66
He Is Jehovah	Betty Jean Robinson	SFPW, 227
He Is Lord	(Traditional)	SFPW, 122
He Is Our Peace	Kandela Groves	SFPW, 213
He Whom the Son Sets Free	Martin J. Nystrom	SB#6, 483
His Name Is Life	Licciardello/Gaither	SFPW, 88

Title	Composer	Resource
Holy Spirit, Thou Art Welcome	Rambo/Huntsinger	SFPW, 133
Hosanna	Carl Tuttle	SFPW, 82
How Great Our Joy!	(Traditional)	TCH, 269
How Majestic Is Your Name	Michael W. Smith	SFPW, 14
I Am Not My Own	Martin J. Nystrom	SB#6, 491
I Am the God That Healeth Thee	Don Moen	SFPW, 232
I Come to the Cross	Somma/Batstone	PHC, 122
I Exalt Thee	Pete Sanchez, Jr.	SFPW, 18
I Extol You	Jennifer Randolph	SFPW, 78
I Live	Rich Cook	SFPW, 124
I Love You, Lord	Laurie Klein	SFPW, 72
I Will Celebrate	Linda Duvall	SFPW, 147
I Will Enter His Gates	Leona Von Brethorst	SFPW, 168
I Will Worship You, Lord	Daniel Gardner	SFPW, 21
I'm So Glad	(Unknown)	SB#6, 495
In His Presence	Dick & Melodie Tunney	SFPW, 46
Jehovah to Me	Cloninger/Keesecker	SFPW, 231
Jehovah, Jireh	Merla Watson	SFPW, 228
Jesus Is My Lord	(Unknown)	SFPW, 54
Jesus, Come/Emmanuel	Townley/McGee	CC, 23
Jesus, Draw Me Close	Rick Founds	PHC, 209
Joy to the World	Watts/Handel	CC, 31
Joyful, Joyful, We Adore You	Johnson/Beethoven	TCH, 271
King of Kings	Conty/Batya/Traditional	SFPW, 94
Let the Peace of Christ	Denny Cagle	SFPW, 251
Let There Be Praise	Melodie & Dick Tunney	SFPW, 250
Let Your Spirit Rise within Me	Randy Speir	SFPW, 235
Let's Worship and Adore Him	(Traditional)	TCH, 247
Lift Up Your Heads	Steve Fry	SFPW, 127
Like a Rose in Winter	Hanson/Murakami	CC, 24
Like a Shepherd	Moen/Simpson	C&W, 112
Lord, I Lift Your Name on High	Rick Founds	CCB, 36
Love Has Come!	Bible/Traditional	TCH, 256
My Peace	Keith Routledge	PHC, 53
Near to the Heart of God	Cleland B. McAfee	UMH, 472
O Little Town of Bethlehem	Brooks/Redner	CC, 26
Of the Father's Love Begotten	(Traditional)	UMH, 184
Oh, How He Loves You and Me	Kurt Kaiser	SFPW, 113
Only by Grace	Gerrit Gustafson	CCB, 42
Open Our Eyes, Lord	Robert Cull	SFPW, 199
People of God	Wayne Watson	SFPW, 139

Title	Composer	Resource
Sanctuary	Thompson/Scruggs	CCB, 87
Shine, Jesus Shine	Graham Kendrick	SFPW, 142
Sing and Be Glad in Him	Lynn DeShazo	SB#6, 525
Sing Unto the Lord	(Unknown)	SFPW, 23
Spirit of the Living God	Daniel Iverson	SFPW, 131
Spirit Song	John Wimber	CCB, 51
Stand Up	(Unknown)	SFPW, 31
Step by Step	Beaker	CC, 63
Surely the Presence	Lanny Wolfe	SFPW, 243
Sweet, Sweet Spirit	Doris Akers	SFPW, 136
The Joy of the Lord	Alliene G. Vale	SFPW, 229
The King of Glory	Jabusch/Traditional	Celebration
The Lord Is My Light	Jeff Nelson	SFPW, 209
The Spirit of the Lord	Billy Funk	C&W, 168
The Steadfast Love of the Lord	Edith McNeill	SFPW, 185
They'll Know We Are Christians	Peter Scholtes	CCB, 78
To a Maid Engaged to Joseph	Grindal/Edwards	UMH, 215
Water of Life	Cathy Townley	CC, 79
We Bring the Sacrifice of Praise	Kirk Dearman	SFPW, 1
We Celebrate	Till/Davenport	SFPW, 162
We Will Glorify	Twila Paris	SFPW, 68
What Child Is This	Dix/Traditional	UMH, 219
When I Look into Your Holiness	Wayne & Cathy Perrin	SFPW, 71
With All My Heart	Babbie Mason	SFPW, 187
Worthy, You Are Worthy	Don Moen	SFPW, 81
You Are My Hiding Place	Michael Ledner	SFPW, 230
You Are	Graham/Townley	CCB, 23
You Who Are Thirsty	Barbara Ross	SFPW, 219